365 WAYS
TO LIVE
CHEAP

YOUR EVERYDAY GUIDE TO SAVING MONEY

365 WAYS TO LIVE CHEAP

TRENT HAMM
FOUNDER OF THESIMPLEDOLLAR.COM

AVON, MASSACHUSETTS

Published by
Adams Media, a division of F+W Media, Inc.
57 Littlefield Street, Avon, MA 02322. U.S.A.
www.adamsmedia.com

ISBN 10: 1-60550-042-9
ISBN 13: 978-1-60550-042-3

Printed in the United States of America.

J I H G F

Library of Congress Cataloging-in-Publication Data
is available from the publisher.

This publication is designed to provide accurate and authoritative information
with regard to the subject matter covered. It is sold with the understanding that
the publisher is not engaged in rendering legal, accounting, or other professional advice. If legal advice or other expert assistance is required, the services
of a competent professional person should be sought.

   —From a *Declaration of Principles* jointly adopted by a Committee of the
American Bar Association and a Committee of Publishers and Associations

Many of the designations used by manufacturers and sellers to distinguish their
product are claimed as trademarks. Where those designations appear in this
book and Adams Media was aware of a trademark claim, the designations have
been printed with initial capital letters.

This book is available at quantity discounts for bulk purchases.
For information, please call 1-800-289-0963.

CONTENTS

WHERE DOES YOUR MONEY REALLY GO?

Do you know where your money goes? Are you really aware of every red cent you're spending, or does a lot of it slip right through your fingers, leaving you wondering at the end of the month how you're going to make ends meet? Knowing where every penny goes is one of the key principles of living cheap. Take this quick quiz to find out how your dollars stack up.

1.	When you look at the receipt after leaving the grocery store, you:
A.	Feel shocked at the total and express disbelief that you could have spent that much.
B.	Feel alarmed at the rising grocery prices, but feel that you made sensible purchases.
C.	Smile happily at your tiny total, knowing that you got the food you needed for the week at a minimal cost.
2.	When you sit down to pay bills, you:
A.	Hope that there will be money in your account to cover the checks.
B.	Get through the task as quickly as possible, but don't worry about having enough money to pay the bills.
C.	Look for ways to trim a few dollars off every bill you pay.

3.	When an unexpected bill comes in the mail, you:
A.	PANIC!
B.	Calmly take a little out of savings and a little out of the checking account and pay the bill, then use the credit card to cover regular expenses for the next week.
C.	Fire off that payment without thinking twice thanks to cheap living and an emergency fund.
4.	It's Sunday afternoon and time to go grocery shopping. You:
A.	Jump in the car and head straight to the supermarket.
B.	Make a grocery list.
C.	Use the grocery store flyer to plan your meals for the week and then make a list from that meal plan.
5.	How much money is in your checking account right now (without peeking!)?
A.	I have no idea.
B.	I know within a few hundred dollars.
C.	I know within a few dollars.
6.	How much money did you spend on entertainment and hobbies last month?
A.	I don't know—a lot?
B.	I know pretty close to the amount, but it's more than is probably healthy.
C.	Ten bucks or so.

7. A friend calls up and wants to do something fun. You:

A. Go out with your buddy and drop at least $100—or whatever the evening requires to "have fun."

B. Go out with your buddy, but just spend $20 or so.

C. Suggest twenty or so different things to do, none of which cost much of anything at all.

8. Your kids are bored. You:

A. Load 'em up and take them to the mall.

B. Load 'em up and take them to the park and then out for ice cream.

C. Pull out board games, play catch in the yard, and spend the afternoon together at home.

9. When you open up your cell phone bill, you:

A. Grumble loudly about overage charges, extra text message fees, and out-of-plan-area calls, but pay the bill anyway.

B. See a few small additional costs, but pay the bill without sweating it.

C. Rarely see an extra cost, but if you do, call up the cell phone company and make sure it doesn't happen again.

10. You see a new toy/gadget/clothing item you really want. You:

A. Whip out the plastic and buy it immediately.

B. Don't buy it right then, but go home and plan how you can afford it, then buy it next week.

C. Go home and see if it fits in your budget. If it doesn't, put it off until a later date when you really can afford it—if you still want it then, that is.

Scoring

For every A answer, give yourself 3 points.

For every B answer, give yourself 2 points.

For every C answer, give yourself 1 point.

Do you know where your money goes?

25 TO 30 POINTS: Your money flutters through your fingers and blows away in the wind. Time to buckle down and learn how to live cheap.

18 TO 25 POINTS: You know some of the tactics for living a financially sensible lifestyle, but too much of your cash still slips through the cracks. Time for a tactics refresher.

10 TO 17 POINTS: You're a thrift machine who knows how to save money—and knows the usefulness of discovering new ways to save a penny.

ng Exchange • Never Be an Early Adopter • Insulate Your Water Heater • Start a Garden • Learn to Love Left
ater • Move to a Cheaper Neighborhood • Rent Out Unused Rooms • Check and Replace Furnace Filters • Dro
Bills on Time • Automate Your Savings • Only Wash Full Loads of Dishes or Clothes • Carpool • Air Up All o

THE TEN BIGGEST TIP$ FOR
LIVING CHEAP

1. Take Little Steps, Not Big Ones

Making changes to your everyday lifestyle is hard—that's why so many people try diets and eventually fail. They start off believing that they can make dramatic changes to their life and it works—for a while. Eventually, though, they fall off the wagon and all of that weight they lost comes right back. Cutting back on your spending is much the same. If you go at it with a high level of intensity at first, eventually you'll rebound and go on a spending spree. The best route to success then is to take little steps, not big ones. Find one tactic in this book and focus on just that tactic for a few weeks, incorporating it into your life. Then try another, and then another. Soon, you'll have made that big change you dream about and it will fit as naturally as a glove.

2. Realize That You're Not Alone in This Journey

Some people spend money like it is going out of style, racking up five figures in credit card debt, multiple vehicle loans, student loans, and mortgages, too. If you're struggling with debt and making ends meet, know you're not alone in this experience and that there are people out there who can help you through this, whether it is your family, your friends, or people online who are sharing their experiences. Don't give in to the sense that it is hopeless—there is hope, and there are people who want to help you.

3. Spend Less Than You Earn

Your primary goal each month should be to spend less than you bring in. If you do that consistently, over and over again, your financial situation will improve. There are a lot of ways to make sure you're doing this—an old-fashioned budget, complete abstinence from credit cards, putting some of your income into savings immediately before you even begin to spend it—but they all come down to one rule: Spend less than you earn. The tips in this book will help you with spending less so that you can achieve this goal every month.

4. Calculate How Much You Really Make

Many of the tactics of living cheap seem like a waste of time to many people. "I'm not doing that to save five dollars!" is a common thing to say. If you feel that way, try this experiment:

► First, calculate how many hours you work in a year. But that's not all . . . add to that the hours spent driving to and from work, the hours spent working on stuff at home, the hours spent entertaining and supporting coworkers, the hours spent shopping for work supplies, and so on. If you spend even a sliver of time on a task for your job, count it.

► Next, calculate how much money you earn in a year, including your benefits (you can get that off your paycheck stub). From that, subtract taxes, the cost of commuting (gas, oil changes, wear and tear on the car, and other maintenance), the cost of work clothes, the cost of child care, the cost of other supplies you need to purchase, and so on. Anything that you buy for your job, subtract it here.

► Then, divide the amount you actually earn by the number of hours that you really work. This can be a painful process.

What does that number mean? You can use that as a comparison for everything that you do.

Thinking of buying an expensive gadget? Use that real hourly rate to figure out how much of your life you're giving to your job to get that gadget. Wondering if a money-saving task is worth it? See how much time it will take and how much money it will save.

You'll be very surprised—things like making your own laundry detergent (tip #18) end up earning far more in savings for the time spent than actually going to work will earn you.

5. RECORD EVERY PENNY YOU SPEND FOR A MONTH

Money slips through our fingers in simple and subtle ways. We spend a little here on something forgettable, spend a little there on an unimportant thing, and at the end of the month, it's panic time—we're left with very little money. Spend a month keeping track of every penny that you spend, noting exactly how much you spent and what you spent it on. At the end of the month, go through it and note which expenses were actually essential and which were frivolous. You'll find two things: The need to write your spending down makes you more vigilant against wasteful spending, and the end-of-month review of your records will surprise you when you see how much of your spending was nonessential. Use that information as a springboard to see what you need to work on.

6. MASTER THE TEN-SECOND RULE

Want to curb that leaky faucet of unnecessary spending? Here's a great tactic. Whenever you're in a store and you pick up an item, hold it for ten seconds. During those ten seconds, ask yourself if you really need it and also if that money wouldn't be better used somewhere else. You'll almost always find yourself putting that unnecessary item back on the shelf and walking away, quite proud that you didn't waste your money on something so unnecessary.

7. MASTER THE THIRTY-DAY RULE, TOO

It's useful to use a similar approach with bigger purchases as well. Whenever you pick up an expensive but not immediately essential item (anything that costs more than $20) and decide after using the ten-second rule that you do want to buy it, put it back on the shelf and wait thirty days. If you still remember and want the item in thirty days, then go back to the store and buy it. Most such purchases will float out of your mind long before then. Using this tactic keeps you from making impulsive buys of expensive things that manage to get past your ten-second filter.

8. Keep Track of Your Progress

Each month, figure out how much you earned, how much you spent, and how much you saved that month and record it. Then, try to match that number the following month. This is, in effect, the simplest form of budgeting—you're merely trying to keep your spending under control from month to month. It also lets you see your continual progress. If you were able to live a bit cheaper and put just $50 a month into savings for six months, for example, you now have $300 saved up, showing you that your little changes are really adding up to something big.

9. Talk about Your Money, Especially with Your Partner

Many couples and families have a chaotic approach to money, with each person doing their own thing financially without understanding their partner's goals, desires, and challenges. Often, this results in partners hiding information from each other, such as high credit card statements and other debts, and this not only damages a family's financial situation, but can also damage a marriage. Take the time to sit down for an hour every month or two and go through your complete financial picture with your partner, including both your successes and mistakes. Plan goals together, and actively support each other. If you're single, identify a "money buddy" whom you can be similarly open with. You can support each other in making good spending and financial choices and offer each other advice in difficult situations.

10. Automate Your Savings

One nice thing about saving money is that you end up with more in your checking account over time—the savings slowly build up. For many people, the problem with that is that the extra money is a temptation to spend on unnecessary stuff. The solution is easy—just save automatically. Have your bank set up an automatic transfer of a small amount each week from your checking to your savings—say, $25 for starters. As you get more adept at saving money, increase that transfer amount, and keep saving. That money can help out in emergencies, help with a big payment, or provide the starting material you need to begin investing.

range • Never Be an Early Adopter • Insulate Your Water Heater • Start a Garden • Learn to Love Leftovers
Move to a Cheaper Neighborhood • Rent Out Unused Rooms • Check and Replace Furnace Filters • Drive Car
on Time • Automate Your Savings • Only Wash Full Loads of Dishes or Clothes • Carpool • Air Up All of Your

CHEAP TACTIC$ FOR
APPLIANCES

11. Do the Research

The biggest mistake you can make when purchasing a new appliance is to head right down to the local appliance store and open your wallet. Do some research into different models and find out more about them. How reliable is the model? Does it do a good job at the task you want? Is it energy efficient? What's a reasonable price for that model? You can find the answers to all of these questions on the Internet. Spend half an hour studying archives of *Consumer Reports* or other consumer publications and find out what they say about the appliance you're considering buying. Just find an article covering the appliance that you're looking at, see what the study has to say, and find a few models that are appropriate for you—not whatever models the salesperson at the shop wants you to buy.

12. Reliability Is the Most Important Feature

The number-one feature that you should look at when buying a new appliance is reliability. Paying a bit more now for an appliance that will last twice as long is a great way to save money over the long haul. A $500 washer that lasts ten years is a far better deal than a $350 washer that lasts only five years. Neat features are nice, but reliability is the one feature that will help keep money in your pocket over the long haul.

13. Look for the EnergyStar Logo

After reliability, the most important feature is energy efficiency. Look for appliances that are EnergyStar certified. These appliances use less energy than those without the certification. Also, compare the energy use numbers among models. They're usually stated in kilowatt-hours per year. Every kilowatt-hour costs you about ten cents on your electric bill, so if you can get a model that uses one hundred fewer kilowatt-hours per year, you'll save $10 per year owning that model over its lifetime. That can really add up over the lifetime of an appliance.

14. Consider Last Year's Models

When you're shopping for appliances, most of the models that you'll be shown are the current year's models, but most appliance stores often have last year's models still available in the back, still new and often at a discounted rate. Research last year's models as well (using older issues of *Consumer Reports*) and if you find one of those for sale at a discounted rate, snap it up.

15. Shop Patiently

In order to find the best price for the appliance model you want, you may have to shop at several places. Take your time with this purchase. You're far better off shopping patiently and finding a good price on the model you want than just buying that model at the first place you go, or buying whatever model is on sale at that first store you visit. *Another tip:* When you know you're about to make the move to replace a major appliance, watch the flyers for appliance sellers in your area. If you've done your research, you should know the expected price on the models you want. A sale on that model can really pay off.

16. Use Cold Water for Most Clothes Washing

The Alliance to Save Energy reports that using cold water for most of your clothes washing saves up to $63 per year. That's because 85 percent of the energy used when washing your clothes is used not by your washing machine, but by the water heater. Most clothes that are not intensely dirty are made just as clean in cold water as in hot water, so give it a try, particularly on your underclothes and towels. If you feel like cold water isn't giving your clothes an appropriate cleaning, use a warm pre-soak—just fill your washing machine with warm water and let your clothes soak in it a bit before they're properly washed.

17. Clean Out Your Dryer Lint

Does your dryer seem to not work as well as it once did? Do you sometimes have to run a dryer load a second time because the clothes are still damp? That's not only time consuming, but it's also expensive, and the cause is usually dryer lint. It's easy to take care of the problem—just make sure your dryer's lint trap is clean (use a vacuum cleaner to clean out the lint trap slot) and also make sure that there's no lint caught where the dryer's exhaust leaves your home. You can also pull your dryer out from the wall, disconnect the exhaust pipe, and make sure that it isn't clogged anywhere (and also vacuum inside the dryer through the exhaust hole).

18. Make Your Own
Powdered Laundry Detergent

Laundry detergent costs as much as twenty cents per load, but you can easily make your own powdered detergent at home for as little as two cents a load. Just take a bar of unscented soap and grate it into flakes using a box grater, then mix those soap flakes with one cup of washing soda and a half cup of borax. You can also add one half cup of an oxygen cleaner like OxyClean, but it works fine without it. You can make multiples of this mix and store it in a large tub. All you need for a load of laundry is two tablespoons (or ⅛ cup) of this mix. Leave a small measuring cup right in your storage tub.

19. Air-Dry Your Clothes
Instead of Using the Dryer

An old-fashioned clothesline is one of the best cost-cutting items available to you. At current energy costs, the average dryer eats up forty cents worth of energy each time you run a load. Hanging your clothes on a clothesline reduces that cost to zero. Over many loads, that adds up to a real savings. Don't have an outside clothesline? Hang one across a spare room in your home, or spread the clothes out to dry. The clothes smell better and you save for every five dryer loads you hang up.

20. Don't Use the Stove
When the Microwave Will Do

For many simple purposes, the microwave oven is much more energy efficient than the stove, often using 75 percent less energy for the same task and adding far less heat to your house. Use your microwave for tasks such as boiling water, steaming and browning vegetables, cooking rice, and other water-intensive applications. It can reduce your cooking costs by up to 20 percent.

21. Turn On the Oven Light While Cooking

Whenever you open the door on your oven, as much as 25 percent of the heat inside is lost and a significant amount of energy is used building that heat again, likely extending your cooking time. Instead of losing heat that way, turn on the oven light while cooking and use a meat thermometer in your food. This way, you can look through the glass on your oven and visually inspect the food inside without opening the door and losing significant heat.

22. Only Wash Full Loads of Dishes or Clothes

Instead of just washing clothes or washing dishes when it's most convenient, wait until the loads are truly full before running a cycle. Appliances are designed to handle full loads, so running partial loads

---

is a sure way to let money float out of your pocket. According to the Rocky Mountain Institute, an average washing machine costs $155 per year to use. Reducing the number of loads you wash can add up to real money over time. Want something clean right away? Wash that item individually by hand.

23. USE THE SHORT CYCLE

Similar to the idea behind washing only full loads, consider using short cycles on your dishwasher and washing machine, especially when the items that you're washing aren't particularly dirty, such as work clothing that you may wear in an office. Using the short cycle can reduce the cost of an individual load by up to 50 percent depending on the model, so get in the habit of using the short cycle for most of your machine washing needs.

24. MAKE YOUR OWN DISHWASHING DETERGENT

Dishwashing detergent can be made at home with common cleaning supplies. Just mix one cup of borax and one cup of baking soda in a tub. Some harder water situations may require the addition of a cup or two cups of powdered purchased dishwashing detergent. Just put in two tablespoons of the powder mix (⅛ cup) into your dishwasher for each load and save about fifteen cents per load. *Another tip:* Instead of using Jet Dry in the rinse cycle to make your dishes dry, use a couple caps full of vinegar instead. Much cheaper, same effect.

25. Don't Install Your Refrigerator
Next to Your Dishwasher or Oven

Many kitchens have this as the default layout, but if you can avoid it, your energy bill will thank you greatly. The natural heat produced by your dishwasher or oven can add heat to the refrigerator if it's placed nearby, causing the refrigerator to run more frequently to maintain the low temperature. If you can, look for a kitchen layout that places the refrigerator far away from the dishwasher or the oven, allowing your refrigerator to be significantly more energy efficient—and thus easier on your wallet.

26. Set Your Refrigerator to the
Warmest Setting; Adjust from There

Many people have their refrigerator and freezer settings much colder than they actually need them to be to keep their food chilled. Instead of keeping your dials turned to the coolest settings, try the opposite—turn them as high as they can go and see how it meets your needs. If you need to, slowly adjust the temperature downward. A reasonable setting on your refrigerator and your freezer can save significant money over time, as your compressor will kick on much less often and thus save money on energy costs. *Another tip:* Pull out your refrigerator every six months and vacuum out the back of it, making sure to clean dust from the coils. This will keep your refrigerator running as efficiently as possible.

27. INVEST IN A DEEP FREEZER

If you have space (in your kitchen, garage, or basement), invest in a deep freezer. A deep freezer allows you to buy your food in bulk, saving significant amounts of money. For example, by contacting a meat locker directly, you can purchase meat in large quantities directly from the provider, filling up your freezer with meat discounted at 30 percent or more compared to what you'd pay at the meat counter at the grocery store. See a great deal at the store? You can stock up big time, putting the excess in the freezer for later use. The use of a deep freezer can save approximately 15 percent on your annual food bill without a major increase in your energy use.

28. START AN AUTOMATIC
APPLIANCE REPLACEMENT FUND

One of the "sneaky" expenses that often starts people sliding down a slippery slope into debt is the unexpected failure of an essential appliance, often at the worst possible time. This usually means that people run out and buy a new appliance on credit without having the money to pay the bill. They are then running short for the next year or so as they pay off that extra bill—and hoping nothing else goes wrong while they're paying it off. Here's a better solution: Take tip #10 and put it to use. Put aside a tiny amount, $10 a week, toward appliance replacement. You've probably already saved that $10 a week by using other tips in this book. If you start doing it now and your refrigerator fails in a year, you'll have $520 already in hand to pay that bill. If the water heater fails two years after that, you'll have $1,040 in hand to cover that bill. All it takes is $10 a week, and if you set up the transfer to be automatic, you'll never notice it—until you need it, that is.

Change • Never Be an Early Adopter • Insulate Your Water Heater • Start a Garden • Learn to Love Leftovers
Move to a Cheaper Neighborhood • Rent Out Unused Rooms • Check and Replace Furnace Filters • Drive Car
on Time • Automate Your Savings • Only Wash Full Loads of Dishes or Clothes • Carpool • Air Up All of Your

CHEAP TACTIC$ FOR
AUTOMOBILES

29. FOCUS ON RELIABILITY AND FUEL EFFICIENCY

It's easy to get excited about all the latest features when you're considering a car purchase, but instead of focusing on the DVD player or leather seats, focus on these buying tactics instead:

► Do your research before you go near a car dealership. Examine the most recent car-buying issue of *Consumer Reports*, for starters, and carefully study their findings on reliability as well as their overall conclusions. Cars marked as highly reliable have significantly lower expenses for repairs over the lifetime of the car, directly saving you cash.

► Focus on buying late-model used cars, as they often have the best long-term value for the dollar.

► Put a high emphasis on fuel efficiency. Over 75,000 miles of driving, a 15 mpg car guzzles 5,000 gallons of gas, while a 20 mpg car only uses 3,750 gallons. At $4 per gallon, that's a savings of $5,000—and that's if gas prices hold steady.

► Know your numbers before you go. Use the Kelley Blue Book (*www.kbb.com*) to find out the value of your current car (if you're planning on trading) and the value of the car you're looking at. You will then have a sense of how fair the offer is.

30. READ THE MANUAL

Your car's manual is a treasure trove of tips and bits of information that can save you a lot of money over the long haul. It should be your primary source for information about how to care for your car and maximize its lifespan. Most of the information available through popular culture about automobile care and maintenance is placed there by organizations wanting to maximize their profits by convincing you that you need maintenance, replacements, and upgrades far more frequently than you actually need them. Read the next few tips and see how often the car manual comes into play to save you money.

31. DON'T BUY A SERVICE CONTRACT OR AN EXTENDED WARRANTY

When you try to make an automobile purchase, the dealer will often try to encourage you to purchase a service contract or an extended warranty on your new vehicle. Say no. If you're interested in such plans, you can shop around for a low-cost service plan. If you're concerned about a warranty, you can purchase one directly from a warranty provider such as Warranty Direct without paying the additional dealer markup. Plus, it gives you time while your basic warranty is in place to do the research and pick out the warranty that's right for you—and it will be far cheaper than what you'd buy at the dealership.

32. AIR UP ALL OF YOUR TIRES

Airing up a car tire is a very simple free procedure that takes only a couple of moments, yet can save you a bundle over time. According to the Car Care Council, a mere 1 PSI drop in air pressure in all four tires can reduce your gas mileage by 0.4 percent, and your car can easily be 10 PSI low without even noticing it—a 4 percent reduction in gas mileage. Over 10,000 miles in a 20 mpg car with gas at $4 a gallon, you can save yourself $80 by just airing them up. Look inside your car's manual to find out the recommended maximum pressure for tires on your automobile and also to find out details on the exact procedure to follow.

33. BUY THE CHEAP GAS

The idea that you need high-octane gas for your car is mostly a relic from the days of older cars that could actually maximize the use of higher-octane gas. Today, most cars run just fine on low-octane fuel. Check your owner's manual to see what the recommendation is for your car and buy the cheapest you can within that recommendation. If buying cheaper gas saves you ten cents per gallon on a 20 mpg car, over the course of 10,000 miles, you'll save $50 in lower gas bills.

34. DON'T GET AN OIL CHANGE EVERY 3,000 MILES

The mantra for oil changes is that you should get one every 3,000 miles, and most car owners quickly run off to get that oil change right on schedule. You might be surprised to find that the owner's manual suggests an oil change every 5,000 miles or, on some models, even less frequently. In fact, 5,000 miles is the recommendation from *Consumer Reports* as well as the guys from NPR's *Car Talk*. If you drive your car for 60,000 miles while you own it, just following the factory recommendations saves you eight oil changes.

35. Use the Manufacturer's Maintenance Schedule

Let's get this straight: Regular maintenance on your automobile is very important for keeping your car reliable and reducing repair costs, and it should be done exactly in accordance with the schedule that the manufacturer recommends. When you buy a car, most dealers will attempt to get you to subscribe to a maintenance schedule through their dealership and will tell you with dead seriousness that you need to follow that schedule to a tee. Often, that's not true—most dealer maintenance routines get you into their auto shop far more often than you need to be. Again, flip open that owner's manual, find the maintenance schedule information, and follow it yourself for all aspects of your car, from brake pad replacement to tire replacement.

36. Minimize Your Load

When you're driving on the highway, most of your engine power goes toward overcoming air drag—the resistance that the air is putting on your car. When you have extra items on your car, such as stuff bundled to the roof or even a ski rack, you're reducing your gas mileage by as much as 5 percent. Similarly, excess weight in your car reduces your gas mileage, so if you're using your trunk as a storage unit, you'll save yourself a significant amount by getting that stuff out of the car.

37. PRACTICE GOOD GAS CONSERVATION HABITS

It's often the little things that really add up, and with gas at more than $4 a gallon, it adds up to big money fast. Here are five more fuel conservation tips that individually won't save a significant amount, but over time and done in combination can save quite a bit of gas expense.

- ▶ Tighten the gas cap as tightly as you can when you finish filling up. Gas evaporates rather quickly, and a loose cap allows that evaporated gas to simply drift out of your tank.
- ▶ Don't top off the tank. When you do, you dramatically increase the chance for gas to slosh out, and when gas prices are high, even a bit of sloshing is money gone from your pocket.
- ▶ Don't rest your left foot on the brake while driving. Even a slight accidental bump of the brake will cause some drag and some additional gas use—plus it'll increase the wear on your brake pads.

► Turn off the air conditioning as you approach your destination. When you're ten or fifteen minutes away from where you need to be, turn off your air conditioning. This will improve your car's mileage and the cab of your car won't get warm enough during that period to cause any discomfort.

► Use appropriate tires for the weather. Snow tires in the summer significantly reduce your gas mileage.

38. USE PUBLIC TRANSPORTATION

If you live in an area where you have easy access to public transportation, use it. Use it to commute to work, to attend social and cultural events, and to run errands. The cost savings of using public transportation is tremendous if you get into a habit of using it consistently. If you can use the bus or the rails to take a trip for $2 when you would otherwise have to drive your car, burn two gallons of gas, pay for parking, and add extra miles onto the car that push you closer to maintenance, the choice is pretty easy.

39. CARPOOL

If you have an opportunity to share a ride to and from work with someone, jump on it. The cost savings of carpooling is tremendous. If your commute causes you to burn two gallons of gas and put forty miles on your car, just two days a week of riding with someone else can put the savings per month well over $100. Carpooling can also add some time savings to the picture as well if you have access to the

HOV lane. If you work in a large organization, it's pretty easy to get a carpool started. Send out an e-mail to as many coworkers as you can stating that you're interested in starting a pool from your area and see how many responses you get.

40. Use a Bicycle

Most nearby trips, such as a trip to the post office or a trip to the local grocery store, are very short—just a mile or two each way. They're also full of stop-and-go driving, which is the least efficient kind of driving for an automobile. Instead of driving, get a used bicycle and use it for these short little trips. Install a small basket on the front so you can easily carry a couple bags of groceries or a package to be mailed. It's a free mode of transportation, doesn't take much longer than a car over a short trip, and is a good way to get a bit of exercise, too.

41. Eliminate One of Your Cars Entirely

If you find yourself using your bicycle and public transportation frequently, you'll likely find that one of your automobiles is being used less and less. Consider selling it. Not only will you make some money from the sale, but you'll have a smaller car insurance payment and no license costs to worry about either, plus you may free up some garage space that can be put to better use in other ways. This is a big step, but it's one that can save you a ton of money on a monthly basis.

42. Don't Speed—Instead, Use Cruise Control

It's tempting to speed when you're driving somewhere, particularly when the commute is long, but speeding is an incredibly expensive tradeoff. It reduces your fuel efficiency, making the trip itself cost more. It puts more wear and tear on your automobile, increasing the chances of a necessary repair. It also increases the chance of an accident, as speeding gives you less time to react. If that's not enough, you also run the danger of being issued a speeding ticket, which has not only a direct cost but can raise your insurance rates as well. The costs of speeding, both potential and real, just to save a few minutes on a trip aren't worth it. Instead, just set the cruise control to the speed limit for long driving stretches; this will keep you from being tempted to speed.

43. Don't Get Optional Stuff During Maintenance

Often when you take your car in for maintenance, the workers inside will attempt to sell you additional products and services, such as replacement windshield wiper blades or a new air filter. Never buy them there. The cost they charge you for a new blade or a new filter, plus the cost for the minute's worth of work to install them, is far beyond reasonable. Instead, go to a discount auto parts store and buy these items yourself, then use the car's manual to install them. You'll not only save a lot on the part itself, but you'll save on the labor cost.

44. Shop Around for Car Repairs

When your car needs repairs, don't simply take it back to the dealership. Pull out the yellow pages (or check out Google Maps) and call several nearby auto repair facilities. Look for those that are ASE (Automotive Service Excellence) certified. You should also consult any of your friends who have knowledge about cars and ask if they have any recommended repair shops. If your car is under warranty, make sure the repair shop will honor that warranty. This will go a long way toward getting you a quality auto repair for a much cheaper price.

45. Pay for Car Repairs with a Credit Card

When you get your car repaired, pay for the repair with a credit card and then pay the credit card balance off immediately. Why? Credit cards offer significant consumer protection against fraud. If your car repair is faulty, you can contact your credit card company and have them deal with it rather than trying to fight it yourself—and likely coughing up more dough for more repairs.

46. Plan Ahead for a Car Replacement

If you want to replace your car as cheaply as possible, the best time to start thinking about it is the day you purchased the previous model. Start putting a small amount away each month automatically (see tip #10) and forget about that amount until your next car purchase. Putting $50 away each month into a 3 percent APY savings account gives you $4,000 toward your next car purchase after six years. That, plus a trade-in, is enough to let you drive off the lot with a very tiny loan. Putting away $100 a month will give you $8,000 after six years, likely more than enough to allow you to trade in your current car and then drive off the lot with a late-model used car without taking out a loan—no car payments at all.

ng Exchange • Never Be an Early Adopter • Insulate Your Water Heater • Start a Garden • Learn to Love Le
ter • Move to a Cheaper Neighborhood • Rent Out Unused Rooms • Check and Replace Furnace Filters • P
Bills on Time • Automate Your Savings • Only Wash Full Loads of Dishes or Clothes • Carpool • Air Up All

CHEAP TACTIC$ FOR
BANKING AND INVESTING

47. GET A BANK CARD WITH A VERY
LARGE FEE-FREE ATM NETWORK

Ever stood at an ATM and seen that dreaded message "This bank charges a $2 fee for use of this ATM"? If you have, blame your bank. In order to cut corners, they've decided to exclude ATMs from their network. Your bank should always have the widest ATM network possible. If you find yourself seeing those messages regularly, that adds up to significant cash straight out of your pocket. Talk to your bank and make sure that you at least have a debit card with a MasterCard or Visa logo on it so you can use it as a credit card. Often you're able to use it as a debit card in the checkout lane and use it to get cash back.

48. GET A CHECKING ACCOUNT THAT OFFERS
MORE THAN 1 PERCENT INTEREST

If you keep your checking account at a bank that does not offer any interest on your checking account, or offers far less than 1 percent interest, look elsewhere. Many banks offer 1 percent or higher interest rates on their checking accounts, meaning they'll actually pay you money for just having your account there. Ask if your bank has an interest checking account and switch to that account. If not, you may want to look at tip #52.

49. Get a Savings Account That Offers
More Than 3 Percent Interest

Similar to tip 48, if the savings account your bank offers doesn't offer at least 3 percent interest, ask them if there is one available that offers that much. Many banks offer rates at 3 percent or above, particularly banks that focus on online services. If you can't get a savings account at your local bank offering rates that high, consider switching to one that does and include online banks in that decision. See tip #52 for more details.

50. Don't Tolerate These Four Fees

Check your most recent bank statement. Do you see things like maintenance fees, mysterious monthly fees, check cashing fees, minimum balance fees, or other fees that seem inexplicable to you? These fees are unnecessary and cost you money. Call your bank and ask to have them waived. If they refuse, then it's time to start looking for a bank that respects you as a customer (see tip #52).

51. Make Sure the Bank's Hours Match Yours

If your schedule makes it difficult to conduct business with your bank and they don't offer online services to help out with basic tasks, then your bank is costing you money. Every time you can't get a check cashed, can't get a transfer set up, or can't do any other business you might want to routinely do, your bank's business practices are interfering with your financial life. Don't accept it. Your bank should have hours that match your schedule and/or online services that help you out with most of these basic tasks.

52. IF YOU CAN'T GET THESE FEATURES, START SHOPPING FOR A NEW BANK

So, the last four tips identify basic features you should be expecting from your bank. Without them, your bank is costing you money. Most likely, your bank doesn't have all these things, but there are many banks out there that offer most if not all of these features. Here are some tips for finding a new bank and making the move to a new account.

► Use Bankrate.com to identify banks with good services. Bankrate. com identifies banks that offer high-interest checking and savings accounts. Click on the "Checking and Savings" tab there to find out all the info you need about your local banks.

► Consider online banks like INGDirect.com. An online bank doesn't offer a brick-and-mortar place to do your bank business, but they generally offer all of the services that a bank can offer through their online services or through ATMs. Even better, since they don't have to pay for a physical location, they can offer great interest rates and no fees.

► If you decide to move to a new bank, leave your old account open for a while to help with the transition. You may have many automatic deposits and other transfers that you may have forgotten about, so leave the old account open for a while to catch these. When you're confident that all of your business has been switched to the new bank, you can close the old bank accounts that were draining your pocketbook and move on with your life.

53. Opt Out of "Courtesy" Overdraft Protection

Many banks offer a "courtesy" overdraft protection service where they offer to cover any overdrafts you might make, which sounds like a good deal at first. It's not. You're usually better off bouncing the check. The program at many banks usually charges you a sizable overdraft fee (usually $35 or so), then charges you a daily fee for each day you're over ($2 to $10 a day). An overdraft check can quickly rack up as much as $135 in fees if you don't cover it in ten days. It's usually much cheaper to just deal directly with the business that you wrote the bad check to. They may charge you a small fee, but if you make it right with them, it'll usually be far cheaper than paying the fees your bank will charge you.

54. Learn How to Use Online Banking

Many banks are now offering online banking services that allow you to use your computer to track your account balances, check your recent transactions, and pay bills directly without writing a check. Learn how to use this service, as it can save you money in many different ways.

- If you're unsure of your account balance, you can log in and check your current standing and recent transactions, which can save you from an accidental overdraft.
- If your bank offers online bill pay, you can save money on stamps. If you can move ten monthly bills from paper checks to online bill pay, that's a savings of $4.20 every month.
- You can avoid late fees by scheduling your regular bills to be paid automatically. No more remembering to pay a bill on time.

55. BALANCE YOUR CHECKBOOK AS OFTEN AS POSSIBLE

If you're not ready to make the move to online banking, you should definitely make sure to balance your checkbook every month, as it can save you from a potentially devastating bounced check or over-draft fee. It's really quite simple; just make sure the statement your bank provides matches your own records. Find a point where you're sure both are right and work forward from there, making sure each payment is accounted for by both you and by the bank. As long as your records and the bank's records stay in alignment, you can be much more confident that you won't "accidentally" overdraft.

56. IF YOU DO OVERDRAFT FOR THE FIRST TIME, ASK FOR THE FEE TO BE WAIVED

Everyone makes a mistake once in a while; sometimes that little mistake can result in an overdraft. If you're a regular customer, this is a fee that should easily be waived if you handle it appropriately. First, make sure that you have sufficient funds in the account to fully cover the overdraft check (and any others that may be outstanding). Then, call the bank's customer support line, confess your mistake, and ask that the fee be waived. If they say no, do not get upset. Ask to speak to a supervisor. If that person won't waive it, try the same procedure at your local branch office. Start by asking the teller, then moving up to the supervisor if you hear a negative answer. Be polite, dress well, and don't get angry if you still hear a negative answer. Quite often, one of the four people you talk to will waive your fee, and like that, you've saved yourself $35. Variations on this approach work well for any kind of fee.

57. OPEN UP A 401(K) OR 403(B) NOW

If your workplace offers you a 401(k) or 403(b) retirement plan and you haven't signed up, do it now. Don't wait another second to do so—it can save you far more money in the long run by starting now than by putting it off. A few pointers:

- ► If your employer offers to match your contributions, contribute as much as you have to in order to get that full match. This is free money from your employer that you don't have to pay taxes on until retirement. Take it if they're giving it to you!
- ► If you're worried that your paycheck can't take a 5 percent or 10 percent hit, don't worry—a 10 percent contribution won't actually

reduce your paycheck that much. This money comes out before taxes, meaning that the percentage of your check that goes toward income taxes right now will actually go down. If you start contributing 5 percent of your check, for example, you'll only actually see a 3½ to 4 percent drop in your actual take-home pay.

58. USE A SIMPLE METHOD
TO CHOOSE INVESTMENT OPTIONS

When signing up for a retirement account, the choices can be overwhelming. Keep it simple; here's what you need to know to get started now (you can always learn more later on).

► If you have the option of choosing a plan that targets a specific retirement date (often called something like Target 2040), choose the one that comes closest to the year you expect to retire and put everything into that one fund.
► If you don't have such an option available, take your estimated retirement age (if you don't know, use 70), subtract your current age from that, and multiply that by two. Put that percentage in the stock fund with the best returns and the rest in a bond fund with the best returns (ask for help if you don't know). For example, if you're 30 and you want to retire at 70, you should put 80 percent into stocks and 20 percent into bonds. If you're 50, you should put 40 percent into stocks and 60 percent into bonds. Then, every five years, adjust the amounts by refiguring

how your split should go. This is a simple rule of thumb that will put you on the safe side.

59. Contribute Regularly to That Retirement Account

When you first sign up, you'll be asked to put down a percentage contribution. Choose a realistic amount. Don't pledge more than you think you can easily swallow. When you've signed up, don't interrupt the contributions. The little sacrifices you make now to keep the contributions going will enable you to have a happy life in retirement instead of having to scrape by on a small Social Security check.

60. Automatically Build an Emergency Fund

At some point in your life, disaster will strike. Your car will break down. You'll need a medical procedure. Someone will break into your house. These can be bad news, and financially costly, too, especially if you have to use a credit card to get through it. During those times, you need to have some extra cash on hand. The solution is pretty simple: Start an emergency fund to help you resolve these types of problems. Simply instruct your bank to automatically take a tiny amount out of your checking account each week (say, $20) and put it into a savings account for you. Let the money sit in that account; then, when the going gets rough, you have that cash available to you. It's probably earned a bit of interest, too, which is a bonus. Planning ahead just a little bit right now can make an enormous difference later on.

61. If You Have an Unexpected Windfall, Put It into a CD

If you're in a situation where you have a significant amount of cash on hand—winnings, a settlement, an inheritance, or anything like that—don't touch it at first. Give yourself time to carefully consider what to do with that cash. A smart thing to do is put it into a certificate of deposit at the bank for six months. It'll earn some significant interest there and also give you the hands-off time you need to carefully come up with a plan for your newfound money. Spending it immediately is usually the worst option, particularly if you're not using it to eliminate debt or build your personal wealth.

62. Ignore Freebies Given Just for Signing Up for Financial Accounts

One tactic that many banks like to use to entice you to switch to their bank is the free gift. "Sign up with us and you'll get a free blender!" "Switch to our 'free' checking and you'll get a $75 signup bonus!" Those initial freebies are often hiding something about the account, something that will help them earn their money back over the long haul. Look very carefully at the account they're offering you with that bonus. Often, there are clauses like minimum balances, hefty overdraft fees, no interest at all, a poor ATM network, or other "features" that will cost you more in the long run. If you're going to switch to a new bank, switch because the account itself is good, not because of a welcoming prize. You'll be better off in the long run.

g Exchange * Never Be an Early Adopter * Insulate Your Water Heater * Start a Garden * Learn to Love Left
ter * Move to a Cheaper Neighborhood * Rent Out Unused Rooms * Check and Replace Furnace Filters * Dr
Bills on Time * Automate Your Savings * Only Wash Full Loads of Dishes or Clothes * Carpool * Air Up All o

CHEAP TACTIC$ FOR
CHILDREN AND FAMILIES

change • Never Be an Early Adopter • Insulate Your Water Heater • Start a Garden • Learn to Love Leftovers
Move to a Cheaper Neighborhood • Rent Out Unused Rooms • Check and Replace Furnace Filters • Drive Ea
on Time • Automate Your Savings • Only Wash Full Loads of Dishes or Clothes • Carpool • Air Up All of Your

63. Start Saving for College as Early as Possible—Even Before the Child Is Born

If you're not saving for your child's college education now, get started right away. The amount of money your family will save over the long haul by socking a few twenties away each month starting now can be tremendous. Here are some options to consider:

▶ Make the savings automatic. Set things up so that even a small amount is put into a separate account for your child. Even $10 a month, started at birth and earning just a 5 percent annual return, adds up to $3376 for your child's college education. That amount can make a huge difference if your child attends a local school or a state institution.

▶ Look into a 529 savings plan. These plans allow you to earn a good return on your savings, allow you to automatically put away a specific amount each month, and protect your savings from taxes. Use Google to find out about the 529 plan available in your state or other 529 plans available to you.

64. Use Cloth Diapers

Most people, when they think of cloth diapering, imagine a horrible mess of plastic pants, washer loads full of stinky diapers, safety pins, and other such images, so they stick with disposable diapers. The only problem is that disposable diapers are a continual cost. You have to keep buying more and more diapers, and they're not all that cheap—often at least a quarter per diaper change for disposable. Modern cloth diapering can be quite simple and can save you tremendous money, especially if you plan to have multiple children. *Tip:* Ask for high-quality cloth diapers, like bumGenius as a baby shower gift, so that you're spared the start-up cost.

65. MAKE YOUR OWN WIPES

Baby wipes are another common parenting expense when you have small children in the house, and it's another item you can make yourself for much cheaper. Just mix two tablespoons of baby soap, two tablespoons of olive oil, and two cups of water. Then, cut a roll of paper towels in half the long way and put the paper towels in a baby wipes box; pour the solution on top and swish it around. Alternately, you can just fill a spray bottle with the solution and use small pieces of cloth as baby wipes, which works well if you're cloth diapering as you can just store and wash the diapers and wipes together. Alternately, if you're adept at sewing (or know someone who is), a much more environmentally sound solution is to head down to your local fabric store and buy a large piece of flannel cloth. Take it home, cut it into wipe-size pieces, then sew the edges so that they don't fray, and you have a ton of excellent cloth wipes that you can continually reuse. Just keep a spray bottle with a solution of witch hazel and water in equal amounts to spray down areas, then wipe them down and wash the cloths. It's environmentally friendly and far cheaper than buying bundles of disposable wipes.

66. Shop Yard Sales for Young Children's Clothing

Many children, particularly young ones, outgrow clothes so rapidly that they wear them only a few times before they're too small. Many families deal with this phenomenon by selling these clothes at a yard sale. That's where you can clean up on baby and toddler clothes that have only been worn a few times. If you have a young child, hit the yard sales hard. If you find one with a lot of clothes, offer to buy everything that will fit your child at a reduced price as a bundle. *Tip:* Clean these clothes at a Laundromat before taking them home just to be sure you don't bring home any unwanted pests.

67. Take Advantage of Hand-Me-Downs

Similarly, if you have family members with older children, consider asking them to participate in a family hand-me-down cycle, where clothes are handed down among extended family members from child to child, and then offer to hand down your no-longer-wanted clothes to other younger children in the family. You can go beyond clothes for this, handing down items like bassinets, cloth diapers, and other useful child-rearing materials.

68. Buy Fewer, Higher-Quality Childhood Toys

Many families are often flooded with toys of various kinds for very young children, particularly when fueled by the desire to have "the best" for those kids. In fact, though, the opposite is true: Young children are far better off with only a small number of toys rather than an overwhelming abundance. Minimize your own spending on toys, leaving most of the toy-buying to relatives who may buy your children Christmas and birthday gifts. Encourage them to focus on only one high-quality toy rather than an abundance of cheap toys, as this minimizes health risks and ensures that the toys your child plays with are sturdy and long-lasting.

69. Focus on Buying Open-Ended Toys

Hand in hand with the idea of fewer toys is the idea of open-ended toys—those that encourage creative and imaginative play. Instead of focusing on electronic toys with limited interactivity, look at toys that offer plenty of room for creativity, such as art supplies and quality building blocks. Again, not only are these toys widely considered to be better for your child's cognitive development, but they're also often less expensive, meaning you can either save money or purchase items of high quality for the same price you might spend on "gee whiz" toys. *Tip:* Look for toys that match these criteria at yard sales when you're shopping for the clothes; just be sure to wash the items well when you bring them home.

70. Participate in Babysitting Exchanges Instead of Hiring a Babysitter

Do you have friends who also have children? Consider discussing a baby-sitting exchange with them in order to save money on babysitters.

Offer to watch their children on their anniversary night, for example, in exchange for the same treatment on your anniversary. Or offer to alternate weekends. Do you like to go out with other couples or other parents? Get a cycle going where two or three parents or couples enjoy an evening together while the other couple watches all of the children. This enables you to have many evenings of fun with a reliable parent watching your children—at no cost to you.

71. ENCOURAGE ART SKILLS WITH AN END ROLL OF NEWSPAPER

One of the best undiscovered secrets in many towns is on sale at the office of your local newspaper. Many newspapers often have a few hundred square feet of blank newspaper left over at the end of a large roll, and they will sell this roll of paper to the public for just a dollar or two. Buying one of these rolls can provide a huge amount of paper for your children to draw on to their heart's content for just a fraction of the cost of buying such paper at the store.

72. EXTEND THE LIFE AND VALUE OF CRAYONS

If your children love crayons, they can often wear crayons down to unusable nubs. One great solution to this problem is to collect all of the nubs, then put several of them into an inexpensive small mold (you can get a nice one at the dollar store) and bake them in the oven at a low heat. You can easily make candy cane–shaped crayons that are made up of bits of old crayons, and this new crayon will change colors as you draw with it. If you save up a bunch of nubs and do this with many crayons at once, it can save you the cost of buying a fresh big box of crayons, plus create memorable and unique crayons for your child to draw with.

73. Make Your Own Playdough

Playdough is a wonderful children's toy. Instead of buying it at the store in overpriced containers, though, why not try making it at home (and getting the kids involved, too)? Just mix two cups of flour, two cups of warm water, one cup of salt, two tablespoons of vegetable oil, and one tablespoon of cream of tartar (found in the spices section at the grocery store) in a pot. Warm it up over low heat and keep stirring it until it begins to feel like playdough in your hands (if it's sticky, keep cooking it). Then scoop out a small ball of the dough and knead it in your hands until it's smooth. Want to make it colorful? Make a small hole in the ball and add a few drops of food coloring or a quarter of a tablespoon of a colorful drink mix, then close the hole and knead the ball again. If you want a brighter color, add a bit more—keep trying until you get what you like. Very quickly, you'll have a cheap and very fun toy for your children to play with and it's entirely edible (though it tastes rather salty).

74. Turn Supplies You Have on Hand into Toys

Almost every item in your home can be turned into a compelling toy for children with some imagination at almost no cost to you.

Here are three suggestions:

▶ Turn an old newspaper into a paper airplane contest. Give everyone a few sheets and see who can make the best paper airplane out of the sheets.

▶ Turn pots and pans and wooden spoons into a drum kit. Sit several pots and pans out on the floor, then hit them all on the bottom with a wooden spoon and observe the different noises they make.

▶ Turn strips of waste paper into a piñata. Cut any waste paper you have into strips. Blow up a balloon, tie it off and put a paper clip around the tie-off point, then tie a piece of string to the paper clip. Mix two cups of flour and ten cups of water, then boil the solution for a few minutes until it becomes paste. Start pasting the strips to the balloon, letting it completely dry overnight every four or five layers. After a few days of putting on strips, you'll have a piñata! Color it carefully with markers, then hang it up and let the kids break it.

75. READ TOGETHER AS A FAMILY

Reading is one of the most inexpensive and fulfilling hobbies that a person can have. Encouraging a love of reading in your own children is a great way to put them on the path to economic success. Plan a family reading hour each day, where everyone gathers in the same room to read independently. Then, once every few weeks, go to the library together and have everyone pick out a few books to read during that reading period. Reading time can be an hour a day where your family relaxes, improves themselves, and doesn't spend a dime.

76. MINIMIZE TELEVISION TIME

Where can that hour for reading come from? Take it away from time in front of the television. Not only does television gobble electricity (the average television uses about 150 watts, and the average cable box uses about 70 watts, meaning that it eats a dime's worth of electricity every four and a half hours of use), but it's also laden with advertisements and product placements that encourage you to go out and buy things you don't really need. Replace that time spent in front of the television with other activities.

77. GO OUTSIDE

One good replacement for television use is to simply go outside. Go on a walk together as a family. Play a game of catch in the yard, or try playing tag or touch football. Go to the park together. Go on a hike. Explore. Catch lightning bugs. Wade in a creek. These are all fun things that you can do together as a family in the great outdoors—and they're all free.

78. UTILIZE COMMUNITY RESOURCES

Extend that recreational exploration outside your home by looking for free resources and activities offered by your local community.

Take advantage of the public parks, basketball courts, tennis courts, swimming pools, and playgrounds in your neighborhood. Check out the organized recreational activities as well. Find out if there are any free or nearly free community events of interest. Stop by city hall or your library and ask for a community calendar. Often these are updated monthly. Join a local volunteer group. Your community is full of free entertainment for your whole family if you expand your horizons a bit.

79. SEGMENT THEIR ALLOWANCE

Many families dole out allowances to their children, often giving them a few dollars once a week followed by a pat on the head. The only problem with this is that it doesn't guide children down a healthy path of managing their own money and often parents wind up supplementing a little. Instead, segment their allowance and teach them how to manage on their own. Break their allowance into four pieces and keep it in four separate jars: one for spending now, one for saving for a long-term goal (like an expensive toy), one for sharing with others (like buying a present for Mom's birthday), and one for charity. Not only does this teach them the basics of how to budget, but it also saves you money because they're fully in control of their own spending decisions based on the rules for each jar. You don't need to "slip" them money anymore, because budgeting is part of their learning experience.

80. Share the Thought Process
Behind Your Purchases

Whenever you make a significant purchase, show your children how you came to the decision behind that purchase. Not only is it an opportunity to teach your children how to buy sensibly, but it saves you money as well because it keeps you honest about why you're buying stuff. In other words, if you do the research and pick the item with the best value, you're not only buying the best deal, but you're also creating an opportunity to teach your children how to find the best deal.

81. Resist the Temptations of Soda and Fast Food

Junk food is a common expense for children in American homes today. It's easy to see why: Junk food is convenient, tasty, and often makes kids happy. Resist that urge to take the easy route, though. Instead, buy inexpensive and healthy snacks to keep on hand. Buy yogurt instead of candy. Buy rice cakes instead of potato chips. Not only are healthier options often cheaper, they're also better for you, reducing health care costs over your child's lifetime (and probably improving your own health as well, since there aren't unhealthy snacks sitting around the house tempting you).

82. Involve Children in Frugal Projects, Like Gardening

Quite often, projects that can save a household a significant amount of money take a significant amount of effort. Take gardening, for example. A well-tended garden can easily save a lot of money in reduced food costs. The only problem with a garden is that it requires almost daily effort to tend it well. That's where the whole family comes in. Take everyone out in the garden and have them all weed, plant, fertilize, and water. Teach your children how it can be fun, and at the same time you'll spend quality time with them. You can also challenge them to weeding contests. Or show them how to make little trenches for watering around plants. Let them take charge of certain plants. The key to getting their interest is to get them personally involved with it. Not only will the effort pay off in terms of food costs, but if you can make it exciting, it also becomes a very inexpensive source of entertainment.

83. BE A FRUGAL EXAMPLE

Whenever you are together as a family, put extra effort into showing your children that you don't have to spend money to enjoy yourself. Resist the urge to buy impulse items at the grocery store. Don't stop along the trip for a quick treat on the spur of the moment. Don't declare that you have to buy new clothes every month or two. Use the library for books and movies. Show them how you save money in your day-to-day life and they'll naturally do it, too. Not only will this save you money throughout their teen years, but it will save them money throughout their lives.

CHEAP TACTIC$ FOR
CLOTHING

84. Avoid Clothes That
Require Washing Separately

If at all possible, avoid clothes that require specific methods when washing. Every separate load requires the full cost: the water, the cost to run the water heater, the cost of running the washing machine, the cost of the detergent, and the cost of the other cleaning supplies you use. This can amount to as much as fifty cents for a load, and for a single item that can add up to some serious cost. Instead, avoid individual wash items and instead focus on those that can be washed together.

85. Focus on Clothes That Match Well

If you select modular clothing, items that go well with many other items in your wardrobe, you can easily get away with a much smaller wardrobe. For men, choose jackets, shirts, ties, and pants that easily mix and match. With five items of each, you can have 625 different dress appearances, more than enough to appear well dressed. This permits you to wash all of your clothes at once each weekend, then carefully remix your options for the week. This drastically reduces the amount of clothing you need to own.

86. Shop at Consignment Shops
and Outlet Stores

When you do need to shop for new clothes and need professional and stylish options, start at consignment shops and outlet stores before hitting the mall. Outlet stores sell out-of-season, recently discontinued, and very slightly flawed clothing items at huge discounts, so shop carefully and you can find some amazing deals on excellent items. Consignment shops often contain the wardrobes of people with more money than sense, who empty out their closets after wearing clothes once or twice (or not wearing them at all). Again, it's a great place to look for nearly new items at extremely cheap prices.

87. Hit Thrift and Secondhand Shops in Upscale Neighborhoods

If you're willing to dig a little deeper for bargains, try hitting up secondhand shops and thrift shops in upscale neighborhoods. Look for the most upscale neighborhood around you, then find any such shops in their commercial area and see what's available. You can often find unbelievable bargains on top-quality and rarely worn clothes at such shops. Expanding your horizons a bit can save you a ton of money.

88. Focus on Quality Brands That Hold Up over Time

When you make the active choice to buy fewer clothes, it becomes much more important to buy individual clothes items that hold up well over time. This requires you to do some research. Identify the brands of the sturdiest clothes in your closet, and also do research online to identify fashionably appropriate brands that are also sturdy. If you're unsure about brands you should be looking for, visit the websites of stores that you would ordinarily buy clothes from and identify the brands they sell. Take that knowledge with you when you go thrift shopping.

89. WEAR OLD CLOTHING AROUND THE HOUSE

When your clothes do begin to show signs of wear and are no longer appropriate to wear professionally or on social occasions, relegate them to clothes around the house. That's right, wear old, beat-up dress shirts when you're mopping the floor or working in the garden. These clothes are well made and sturdy and have a lot of life left in them. Keep wearing them until they really are ready to fall apart. That way, you don't have to spend much at all for casual clothes, either—you can keep that cash right in your pocket.

90. BUY CLOTHES OFF SEASON AND ON TAX-FREE HOLIDAYS

If you must buy new clothes, do some careful planning for those purchases. Buy summer clothes for the following year at the end of summer, and do the same for other seasons. Also, plan your clothes shopping for tax-free holidays, where stores compete for the customers that they know will be out and about by offering strong sales. Careful planning can save you a tremendous amount of money on clothes purchases.

91. SWAP CLOTHES WITH SIMILAR-SIZE FRIENDS

Another useful tactic if you like new clothes to wear but don't want to spend the money for more clothes is to swap a portion of your wardrobe with a friend or relative who has similar sizes and tastes as you. Swapping several shirts or pants can make your wardrobe feel fresh and new again, cement a friendship, and save yourself a surprising amount of money.

92. ROTATE CLOTHES SEASONALLY

Another trick to keep clothes seeming fresh and new for years is to rotate your clothes on a strong seasonal basis. Each spring, box up all of your winter clothes and put them into storage, then unbox your spring and summer clothes. Then, after the season is over, box up your spring and summer clothes and unbox your fall and winter ones. They'll feel fresh and new and make it appear to the people around you that you have a fresh new wardrobe. Not only that, but careful storage and clothes rotation can also extend the lifespan of your clothes significantly, allowing you to keep items seeming new for years.

93. SELL OR DONATE CLOTHES YOU NO LONGER WEAR

For many people with an overstuffed closet, clothes are merely another thing to collect, and collections are almost always directly opposed to living cheap. If you have more clothes than you actually wear on a regular basis, consider getting rid of some of your clothes.

Sell some, or donate some to a charity, making sure to get the receipt for tax deduction purposes. Cleaning out your closet by figuring out what you actually wear and what you don't can both earn some money and also help you get more in touch with the clothes you own. You might realize that you do have plenty of clothes and don't need to buy more.

94. Don't Buy Clothes Simply for the Emotional Rush

For many people, it can feel very good to buy a new article of clothing. It provides something of an emotional rush. That emotional rush is dangerous, as is any strong positive feeling related to buying something. If you get excited at the thought of buying clothes and it gives you a big rush to get something new, recognize that this is a problem and it's extremely unhealthy for your long-term financial shape. Focus instead on other positive experiences that don't revolve around money. Realize that buying something new is merely an exchange of your hard work for a material item when that money could be used to buy your freedom from debt.

95. Don't Wash Clothes That Aren't Dirty

If you wear an item of clothing all day that doesn't get dirty, why wash it? Washing it reduces the lifetime of the clothes item and has a cost in terms of energy use, water use, and cleaning agent use as well. When you get undressed, inspect your outer clothes for cleanliness and, if they're still clean, hang them up for future use. One technique to use is to separate your clothes into "fresh" and "worn once" groups—if you use an item from the "worn once" group, it's time to wash it.

96. Learn Basic Sewing Skills

If you know how to hem a pair of pants, sew a button back into place, and repair a small breaking seam, then you've got the skills you need to fix most of the minor clothes repair issues that might occur. Fifteen minutes with a needle and thread to repair a shirt or make a pair of jeans fit your child can save you $20, so it's well worth your while to learn basic sewing. Don't know where to begin? Look for tutorials online that explain how to do this step by step.

97. Use Household Items You Already Have to Remove Stains

Most minor clothes stains can be fixed with just a few items from around your house. Try this simple solution for stains on furniture, carpet, and light-colored clothes: Make a paste by mixing ¼ cup hydrogen peroxide with ¼ cup baking soda, then spread the paste on the stained area liberally and rub it in deep. Let it sit for fifteen minutes, then rinse the area thoroughly. This procedure can take out sweat stains, mud stains, bloodstains, and many others and is a great (and cheap) first action to take before breaking out more expensive cleaners (or throwing the clothing away). On darker clothing, take a stick of clear underarm deodorant and rub it vigorously on sweat stains. On other stains, try rubbing the area briskly with a slightly damp bar of soap before washing it. These techniques will eliminate the vast majority of stains that you might face without having to buy expensive washing machine additives or pretreatment solutions.

98. CUT DRYER SHEETS IN HALF AND REUSE THEM

Dryer sheets are a great way to reduce static cling and make your clothes smell fresher when they come out of the dryer, but a single dryer sheet can actually help with four loads of laundry, not just one. Just cut the sheet in half and use one of the halves in a load. Then, leave that used dryer sheet on top and use it again for a second load. This can cut down greatly on the cost of dryer sheets while still getting almost all of the laundry-freshening effect.

CHEAP TACTIC$ FOR
CLUTTER

99. Realize That Clutter Itself
Is a Giant Money Sink

Clutter accumulation is one of the biggest money sinks in a house. Unused objects and items, merely saved for "someday" or for faint nostalgic reasons, not only make your home or office appear cluttered and unfriendly to outsiders (reducing the value of your property), but also contain within them value that you're not using elsewhere. A $5 trinket shoved onto a shelf with dozens of other $5 trinkets is $5 that could be used to pay down your debt and make your environment look better at the same time. It's a way to simultaneously earn a profit while decreasing the cluttered look of your home.

100. Sell Specific and Individually
Valuable Items on eBay

The first place to start in the clutter battle is looking at your collections. What do you collect? Where do you keep those collections? Do those collections provide genuine value to you, or do you keep them for reasons you can't really explain? Go through your DVDs, your CDs, your clothes, your collectibles, your video games, and so on, identifying items that you don't have a specific and clear attachment to. Clean out your closets and see what's in there that you actually need. Identify the valuable individual items in those collections and sell the individual items online on eBay or Amazon. Just focus on the items with significant individual value—the bulk, ordinary DVDs and CDs, won't earn you enough to make it worth your while.

101. SELL BULK ENTERTAINMENT ITEMS AT A SECONDHAND ENTERTAINMENT SHOP

What about the remaining bulk items, the unwanted collections of DVDs you'll never watch again and CDs that went out with the '90s? Box them up and take them to your local used media shop. You'll generally get a dollar or two a pop for these items, which you can then use to start saving or pay down your accumulated debt. Even better, your home will have less clutter in it, meaning less maintenance time for cleaning and less effort to make it presentable for guests.

102. HAVE A YARD SALE

Still got items left over? Have a yard sale and price everything to sell. The best yard sale tactic is pricing everything at the same price, then lowering that price at regular intervals throughout the weekend. So, start your yard sale on Friday evening with every item for $2. On Saturday morning, lower it to $1 an item then in the afternoon, go down to fifty cents. On Sunday morning, go down to twenty-five cents; then on Sunday afternoon, go down to ten cents. This will not only help you move all your stuff, it will attract repeat visitors who will elect to come back and try to get that item at a cheaper cost later. This can eliminate a lot of clutter and earn you some extra money as well.

103. DONATE TO GOODWILL

If you're still holding leftover items, donate them to Goodwill or the Salvation Army. Get a receipt and use that on your income tax next year—even a small donation can get you a financial benefit. Plus, those unwanted items will wind up with someone who wants them.

104. Put a "Sell By" Date on It

If you have some items that you're thinking about getting rid of, but aren't quite sure, put them in a box and label the box with a date six months or a year in the future. If that date passes and you've never even looked at the items, it's safe to sell them. After all, at that point the items are no longer an active part of your life and are just taking up space and holding value that you could be putting into saving for the future or reducing debt.

105. Don't Replace Clutter with More Clutter

When you finally do get rid of all of the excess stuff, your home will feel emptier. Don't use that as an excuse to fill it with more stuff just for the sake of having stuff. Instead, enjoy the space. Spread out some projects that you've been thinking of working on. Enjoy more free time now that you don't have to deal with the clutter. Perhaps you'll even realize that you don't need all of the space that you have and look at downgrading your living space, or perhaps bring in a roommate to help share the costs of the rent or the mortgage.

106. Avoid Printed Documents

Many people get several different statements in the mail, often taking up pages and pages of space. These printed documents come at a price. They take up more space in the trash, increase chances for identity theft, and require more time to deal with. Find out whether you can switch to electronic copies of many of these statements. It'll reduce the amount of mail you have to deal with (which can decrease trash pickup costs), reduce the potential threat of identity theft, and perhaps also save you the cost of stamps if you can switch to electronic payments as well.

107. Trim Your Magazine Subscriptions

Another great way to reduce clutter and save money at the same time is to reduce your magazine subscriptions. If you find that you're not keeping up with a magazine subscription and old issues are stacking up, unsubscribe from the magazine and focus on those you actually read. Not only will this reduce clutter around your home, but it'll also save you money to invest elsewhere. *Another tip:* If you hold on to old magazines, go through them and just remove the material from each issue you might use again, then get rid of the issue. It'll free up space and make it easier for you to find information.

108. Borrow Stuff You'll Only Use Once or Twice

If you're considering buying an item that you'll only use a few times, look seriously into borrowing opportunities. Not only will this save you money in terms of buying the item, it also doesn't require the space to keep it around. For media sources, like books and movies and CDs, check out the library. Need some equipment or tools? Ask around the neighborhood (but be willing to lend your own stuff out in return). If you're close with another person in the area, you can even consider "sharing" significant purchases that you won't be using simultaneously, like lawn mowers.

109. Every Time You Buy an Item, Get Rid of One

This is a clever clutter-reduction tactic that keeps you from accumulating stuff and also saves you money. Every time you buy a nonessential item, commit to getting rid of another item you already own. For example, if you decide to buy a nifty new kitchen knife, commit to eliminating another similar knife. If you buy a new book, get rid of a book you already have by giving it to a friend or taking it to a used bookstore. This makes you carefully consider a new purchase and helps to eliminate clutter when you do decide to bring home something new.

110. Start a "Mail Basket" and Process It Weekly

Clutter can sometimes cause additional problems, such as misplacing a bill in the clutter and having to pay a late fee even though you had plenty of money to pay it. The solution is simple: Get a "mail basket" that collects all mail that you receive, then go through it completely once a week and process everything in it. Throw away any junk, pay any bills, handle any correspondence, and so on. If you successfully empty that mail basket each week, you'll never accidentally fall behind on a bill again and you'll never be caught up in a clutter of unhandled mail. *Bonus tip:* Start a filing system for your papers when you start a "mail basket" and handle all filing each week when you go through the basket. That way, you'll always be able to find important papers that may be costly to replace.

111. Go Through the "Clutter Attractors" Regularly

Every home has a few "clutter attractors," spaces where things seem to clutter over time. Like the catch-all drawer, the table near the front door where you toss your keys after a day at work, the bedside table, and the downstairs closet. These places almost always wind up catching little important things, things that you should have acted on, like bill statements or checks to be cashed, and sometimes these things can be forgotten in our busy lives. The remedy for this is to check those clutter-attracting areas regularly. Go through the items you find there and see if there isn't anything important you may have missed. This can easily end up saving you money if you discover a bill that needs paying or a check that needs cashing or a rebate form that needs filling out.

112. Read Your Favorite Newspaper Online

If you get a newspaper delivered every day, consider canceling the subscription and reading it online. Not only does this directly save you money by cutting out the cost of subscribing, but it also cuts down on the clutter in your home and the amount of trash you have to throw away. Many newspapers earn significant revenue from their websites today, so don't worry about hurting the newspaper's bottom line if you unsubscribe and replace it with regular viewings of the newspaper's site.

113. Unsubscribe from Catalogs

Catalogs are just collections of temptations. A catalog in the mail will do nothing more than encourage you to buy things that you wouldn't have otherwise purchased, and an unnecessary purchase is the mortal enemy of living cheap. Unsubscribe from any catalogs that you receive by calling the number in the catalog and requesting removal from their mailing list. Not only will this save you money, but it's also a useful way to reduce the amount of clutter that your house catches.

114. Unsubscribe from Charity Mailings

Another effective method of reducing temptation in the mail is to unsubscribe from charity mailings, particularly those that you do not intend to pledge to in the future. Call their number and ask them to stop their mailings to you, informing them that you'll be planning your charitable giving on a regular basis and will send them gifts of your choosing without the mailings. Giving to charity is a powerful thing, but it's something that's worth the time to carefully plan and budget for, not write out an unplanned and unbudgeted check on a whim. Not only does this reduce the costs for that charity, since they're no longer sending out wasteful mail, but it reduces your clutter and also reduces the chance that you'll send out a check without giving it the thought that charity deserves. Instead, plan your charitable giving well in advance and focus your gifts on charities that really matter to you, not on the charity that happens to send you something in the mail that week.

115. SIGN UP FOR THE DO NOT MAIL REGISTRY AND THE DO NOT CALL REGISTRY

Another effective way to simultaneously reduce clutter and also reduce the potential temptation of direct marketers is to sign up for the national Do Not Call registry, which informs telemarketers that you do not wish to be contacted by telephone regarding their direct marketing efforts. Visit *www.donotcall.gov* to get started. Similarly, there is an ongoing push for a Do Not Mail registry, which you can find out more about at *http://donotmail.org*. At that site, you can sign a petition to enact a national Do Not Mail registry, plus request that participating direct mailers no longer send junk mail to your home (many are happy to oblige because it cuts down on their costs). Both efforts will save you time in the long run and quite possibly save you money, too.

116. Don't Upgrade Your Living Space to House More Stuff

One of the biggest reasons that people consider upgrading their home is that they simply don't have room for all of their stuff. That's the single worst reason to lay out a huge amount of money for a space upgrade you don't actually need. If you're considering upgrading because your stuff is starting to fill up all of your space, take a hard look at that stuff around you and ask yourself how much of it you really need. Then, instead of shelling out a lot of money for bigger housing, put some money in your pocket by getting rid of that unwanted stuff using the tips in this chapter. The less junk you have, the less space you need to live, and the less your housing bill will be.

CHEAP TACTIC$ FOR
CREDIT CARDS AND DEBT

117. FIND YOUR MOTIVATION

Bad spending habits, the kind that result in ever-increasing debt and credit card problems, are usually the child of a bad routine. Humans are beings of habit. We fall into certain routines and it takes a powerful force to knock us out of that routine. To break the habit of consistently overspending and putting things on credit, you need to find that powerful force that motivates you to change. Whenever you go to use the plastic or take out more debt, think about that motivator. Some suggestions: your children (and their future), your dream home, the ability to retire and still have some time to enjoy active life, the shame of having to declare bankruptcy, or the ability to quit your job and chase the career of your dreams. Find that one thing that you want so badly that it hurts, then recall it every time you pull out the plastic. *A great tip:* Glue a picture of that motivation to the front of all of your credit cards, so you have to see it each time you head to the checkout.

118. KNOW WHAT YOU OWE

The first step is to get a grip on your total financial situation. Create a master list of every debt you have, including the total balance on that debt and the interest rate you're being charged. List everything, including credit card debts, student loans, mortgages, car loans, furniture loans, and personal loans. You need to get a complete picture of what you owe before you can start getting rid of your debt. Remember, every dollar you pay in finance charges or interest is a dollar lost. To truly live cheap means to pay no finance charges or interest at all.

119. CONSOLIDATE OR REFINANCE ANY DEBTS

Are there any debts on that list that you may be able to consolidate with others at a lower interest rate? Outstanding student loans are usually a good place to start looking, as consolidation can sometimes significantly reduce your overall interest rate and lower your monthly payment. You may also be able to refinance your home mortgage to a lower rate (if you can lower your rate more than 1 percent in the first five years of your mortgage, it's well worth it), or consolidate many of your high-interest credit card debts into a home equity line of credit. You may even want to look at transferring credit card balances to new cards with a 0 percent balance transfer offer. Your goal should always be to move the highest interest rate debts first; the bigger the gap between your old interest rate and your new interest rate, the better. Remember, though, these are solutions to make repaying your debt easier, not a tool with which to get more easy credit to charge up those cards even higher.

120. VISIT YOUR LOCAL CREDIT UNION

If you don't know where to begin, the place to start is your local credit union. Explain your situation in detail and tell them that you're seeking to move your high-interest debt to something with a lower rate. Credit unions often have many options available and typically have the strongest rates in your local area, plus they often provide free financial advice for a person trying to deal with debt. Consider your local credit union as the first stop when thinking about how to fix your debt situation if it's starting to get out of control.

121. CONFRONT THE CREDIT CARD COMPANIES

If you still have high-interest credit card debts left after such consolidation, it's time to actually start confronting the credit card companies. This isn't unusual, particularly with younger people who don't have many accumulated assets. The first step is to flip your credit card over and call the number on the back. When you get someone on the line, state very clearly that you would like the interest rate on this card reduced because the rate is making it difficult to pay off the card, and that you are considering transferring the balance to another card. If the first person says no, ask to speak to a supervisor, and keep escalating until you hear a positive answer. Rinse and repeat for all of your cards and your finance charges will be greatly reduced, meaning you'll have smaller minimum payments and more breathing room each month.

122. RESIST TEMPTATION TO USE YOUR CARD ONCE YOU PAY IT DOWN

All of these efforts are nice in that they reduce your monthly bills by reducing the interest rates, and likely you'll be able to start paying down your cards faster. If you did some balance transferring, it's also likely that you have a lot of free credit available already. Don't use it. Using credit cards beyond your means is what got you into credit card trouble in the first place. It's not merely a method to allow you to keep living beyond your means. It's an opportunity to get out of the hole and not worry about your debt ever again.

123. SWITCH TO USING ONLY CASH AND CHECKS FOR A YEAR

One method to keep your hands off the credit cards is to switch to using only cash or checks (or a debit card) for all of your purchases for a year. This forces you to get in touch with your money again. Without plastic, you're forced to carefully consider each purchase that you make and verify that you do in fact have enough money for that purchase before you make it. Some ideas:

► Don't destroy your credit cards, but instead freeze them in a block of ice. Just pour a small pan about a third full of water and freeze it. Then toss your credit cards on top of the ice and pour on some more water, then freeze it again. Your cards will be frozen in the middle of that cube, inaccessible unless there's a real emergency; any time you think about getting them, you'll have a long time to consider it as you melt (or break) the ice.

► Remove your credit card numbers from any online sites you use regularly. If you use your credit card for billing on iTunes or on Amazon (or anywhere else), remove your credit card number and, if you must, replace it with a debit card number instead so the money comes straight from your checking account.

124. CONSTRUCT YOUR DEBT REPAYMENT PLAN

The next step to take to get your debt in order is to construct a plan for getting rid of it. Each month, you'll need to make minimum payments on all of your debts, as well as a larger payment on one of the debts. A debt repayment plan is mostly just a decision on the order of debts you'll repay and the amount you'll pay extra each month. The key to the plan is that you'll need to do this without racking up additional significant debt. Here are some ideas:

► The "debt snowball" method was made popular by personal finance radio host Dave Ramsey. With that plan, you always focus on paying off the debt with the lowest balance, so you can feel the success of eliminating debts on a regular basis. When a debt is paid off, you "roll" the payment you were making on that debt (the old minimum plus the extra you were making) into extra payments on the next debt on the list.

► The mathematically optimal method is to focus on paying off the debt with the highest interest rate, regardless of balance, and then "snowballing" the minimum payment onward once you pay off a debt. This method is the best in terms of the amount of money you have to pay overall, but is harder to follow because successes can be few and far between.

125. Try Using the Snowflake Method

Snowflaking is a spinoff of the "debt snowball" method described in #124. A snowflake is merely an opportunity to add a little bit more to your extra debt payment each month. For example, let's say that you usually go to the coffee shop on Monday mornings, but one Monday you decide to skip it. Instead of spending that $7 on a coffee and a bagel, instead you add $7 to your extra debt payment. Did you find $5 in the parking lot blowing in the breeze? Use it as a snowflake and add $5 to your debt payment. Sell something on eBay? Return some aluminum cans (or sell some for scrap metal)? Get a rebate? Receive an "economic stimulus" check or an income tax rebate from the government? Snowflake them all!

126. Know Your Credit Report and What It Means

Countless businesses utilize your credit report to assess how trust-worthy you are. From the obvious (car loans, home mortgages, credit card rates) to the surprising (insurance rates), your credit report (and scores calculated based on the content of your report) has a great deal of influence on the amount you have to pay on almost every-thing. Even worse, errors on your credit report can cause all of your rates to go up, costing you a lot of money. Fortunately, it's easy to find your credit report for free, check for and correct errors on it, and ensure that it remains strong in the future by following these tips:

► You can get your credit report for free, no strings attached, from the federal government at *www.annualcreditreport.com*. This site allows you to exercise your legal right to check your credit report from each of the three major credit reporting agencies once a year. Use this site and download your report so you can know where you stand.

► Correct any errors on your credit report—debts you paid off that aren't reported, stuff that you have never seen before, and so on. Contact the organization that's claiming a debt (their phone number is usually on the report) and get the issue straightened out.

► Don't be late with payments and don't open up credit cards unless there's a good reason for it. Check your credit reports once every year so that you can quickly find out if anything false has popped up on your report.

127. PAY OFF YOUR WHOLE CREDIT CARD BALANCE EACH MONTH

The best tactic of all with credit card usage is to avoid finance charges in their entirety, and you can do that on most cards by paying off the entire balance each month. Every time you carry a balance forward on your card, you're essentially agreeing to hand over money to the credit card company in exchange for nothing more than their permission to not pay the debt until next month. Don't pay that fee—pay off the whole balance instead. If you're spending within your means, this should be easy. It should only be challenging if you're pushing the limits of what you can afford or spending far beyond it.

128. USE A CREDIT CARD THAT ACTUALLY BENEFITS YOU

Once your credit is in good shape and you're not overrun with debt, a credit card can become a tool to make regular purchases much easier and earn some useful rewards. If you get into a healthy routine of paying off your credit card debt each month, then a solid rewards card can be as good as money in the bank. There are many good card offers out there. Look for those that offer mileage bonuses to people who drive a significant amount, or cards that offer strong bonuses at the businesses you already use the most, like specific grocery stores or gas stations. A solid rewards card can earn you 3 to 4 percent in rewards or rebates on your everyday purchases. The key, though, is to pay off your balance every month. If you fail to do that, then you lose the benefits of a rewards card.

129. DON'T SIGN UP FOR STORE CREDIT CARDS JUST FOR THAT ONE-TIME BONUS

Many stores have an in-store credit card that is offered to you at the register, usually with some intriguing pledge like 10 percent off your current purchase. While it's tempting, it's not worth signing up for several reasons. First, the interest rates on in-store cards are often incredibly high, some approaching 30 percent annually. That means that for every $100 you leave on the card, they charge you $30 a year for that service. Second, the card itself tempts you to go back to the store, as it has the store's logo loudly branded on it. When you see it in your wallet, you'll think you can go there and buy more things and not have to actually pay the bill, but the bill comes around later and it's expensive. Third, every time you open a new credit card, you not only get a small negative impact on your credit report, but you also slightly increase your chances of identity theft. Add them up and a store credit card simply isn't worth the $10 or $20 you might save right then.

130. BE ACCOUNTABLE— USE YOUR FAMILY AND FRIENDS

Recovering from debt is a challenge, and it's very easy to slip back into old habits. To keep yourself in check, utilize your family and friends to help you through these challenges. Tell them what you're going through, talk to them when it's tough, and have them help you steer yourself away from spending temptations. The support that family and friends can offer you is tremendous. Look to them as a valuable resource as you learn to truly live cheap.

131. ASK ABOUT FEES WHEN SHOPPING FOR LOANS

If you're in a situation where you're about to acquire a new debt, make sure you understand all of the fees you'll be charged when you get that loan. Many loans are saddled with lots of little fees—ask about all of them. Better yet, ask for them to be waived. If you can get even one or two of the hidden fees removed from your loan, it's worthwhile, and the worst they can do is say no. Take the time and challenge all of those little fees, it can really pay off.

132. Sign Up for Automatic Repayment Plans for Student Loans

Upon entering repayment, many student loans offer a small rate reduction if you sign up for an automatic payment plan. Do it, without hesitation. Not only does it directly save you money (remember, 0.25 percent of $40,000 is $100), but it also helps to ensure that you're never late with a payment, saving you from the cost of late fees. This is one of those rare opportunities where jumping on board with an offer from the company can save you real money, so don't miss out on it.

ing Exchange • Never Be an Early Adopter • Insulate Your Water Heater • Start a Garden • Learn to Love Let
ater • Move to a Cheaper Neighborhood • Rent Out Unused Rooms • Check and Replace Furnace Filters • Dr
Bills on Time • Automate Your Savings • Only Wash Full Loads of Dishes or Clothes • Carpool • Air Up All o

CHEAP TACTIC$ FOR
ELECTRONICS

133. Never Be an Early Adopter

It's always a big temptation to be the first person on your block to be the proud owner of the latest hot item. It's fun to show off that gadget a little, but what's easy to forget is that the privilege of showing off that new item is incredibly expensive. You'll pay a huge extra amount up-front to be one of those early owners, plus the item is much more likely to be fragile and to wear down quickly if it's one of the early versions of the item, meaning it'll have to be replaced that much faster. Instead, if there's a hot new item you're tempted to have, exert a little bit of patience. You'll save yourself the "early adopter fee" and likely have a more reliable version of the item, which will save you even more.

134. Consider Whether You'll Actually Use the Item in a New Way

It's easy to see an item used by someone else and quickly convince yourself that the item will in fact change your life. But step back a minute and ask yourself how this device will actually improve your situation from the current condition. Will this device enable you to do something tremendously new compared to what you can do right now? Or is it just a minor change, like a small increase in display quality or a touch-screen improvement on a device you have right now? If it's just a little change, ask yourself whether that little feature is really worth the high price tag, particularly if it requires you to upgrade lots of other things as well (like the upgrade from videocassettes to DVDs) or requires you to start paying for a service for what you were getting for free (like the upgrade from AM/FM radio to satellite radio).

135. Pick the Model Now, Then Wait Six Months
If you're still convinced that you want a particular item, agree that you will purchase the item in six months if you still want it. Spend that time researching the item, considering whether or not you'd actually use the item, and waiting for the price to come down or a newer version to come out. If you decide that you're going to buy a newer model, start that six-month clock over again. The most likely result of this six-month wait is that you'll either forget about the item or realize that you don't actually need it, in which case you'll have saved yourself a significant amount of money by being patient.

136. Know the Features
You Need Before You Shop
If you're about to sink some money into a new electronic item, know what features you actually need before even beginning to shop. List exactly what you're looking for before you even start looking at research materials. This is much the same psychology as preparing a shopping list before you go to the grocery store. It keeps you focused on exactly what you need instead of being distracted by something else that might come along. Before you even begin to research your purchase, know exactly what you want.

137. Avoid the "Feature Creep"

When you do begin to research your purchase or shop around, you'll often discover nifty features that show up in the higher-end models (often thanks to promotional materials, the overtures of a clever in-store salesperson, or a gadget-loving friend who extols the virtue of some minor, expensive, and nonessential feature). Ignore them. These neat features are not features you need, they're merely features you're being lured into wanting on the spur of the moment. Look for the core features you're interested in and let the rest steal the money from someone else's wallet.

138. Shop Around, Both Online and Off

If you're being patient about your purchase, you'll have plenty of time to shop around very carefully for the item. Look at retailers both online and offline and find the best prices, the best return policies, and the best assistance for questions that you may have about the item. Quite often, online retailers have better prices, but offline brick-and-mortar retailers can have better service and return policies, so consider the value of service and return policies in your purchase. If an item would be difficult to return or may require some service or assistance to install, consider that a valuable premium for buying the item in a store, even if the price is a bit higher. The key is to find the best overall value for your dollar, and that may be online in some situations and offline in others, depending on what you are trying to purchase.

139. Look at Refurbished Models

Many stores offer refurbished models—items that were originally sold and then returned with a minor defect that has now been repaired. These items are often as good as new, but are sold at a discounted price. Do some research into refurbished models available for the item you're looking for. Quite often, you can find refurbished models with the same warranties and benefits as buying new but with a significant discount on the purchase price. If you don't know where to begin, ask. A timely question can often save you money.

140. Ask about Retail Returns or Open-Box Items

Many shoppers will buy an item, take it home, rip open the box, then discover that it's not exactly what they wanted or that it's not compatible with their other equipment. They return it to the store and get their refund, but then the store is often left holding a perfectly new item in a beat-up box, which they're obligated to sell at a discount. If you're about to buy an item in a store, ask about retail returns or open-box items, particularly if what you're looking at isn't the latest and greatest version of the item. You'll often be surprised at how much of a discount you can get on a good-as-new item in a cardboard box with a torn flap.

141. Check for Discontinued/Floor Models

Another way to save on electronics is to check out discontinued models. Many stores will steeply discount brand-new products simply because a product line is being discontinued by the manufacturer, often for reasons that have very little to do with the quality of the item. You can also often find a steep discount in retail stores by buying floor items—those that sat out in the store on display for customers to look at. If you're certain of your feature list and find items in either of these categories that match the features you want, don't hesitate to jump on board, especially if the warranty on the item remains valid (be sure to ask).

142. IF YOU GET A REBATE FORM, FILL IT OUT IMMEDIATELY

It's very easy to get lured in by a stellar price on an electronics item, only to discover that the low price is only that low due to a rebate. Retailers and manufacturers love to use the rebate as a method to make a price appear lower than it really is, because shoppers sometimes fail to send in their rebate form. Quite often, it's because they simply forget about it. It's another little task to do, one that's easy to toss in a clutter attractor and forget about. The solution to that problem is simple: Fill out that rebate form as soon as you can, even in the car before you leave the store. Make it your goal to get it in the mail by the end of the day or else the likelihood that you'll forget about that money will vastly increase, and a rebate form discovered after the expiration date is not worth anything at all.

143. SEND IN THE REGISTRATION FORM
IMMEDIATELY—BUT DON'T FILL IT OUT COMPLETELY

Most electronics products (and many other products) include a registration form that they ask you to send in. Quite often, you're required to send it in to activate the warranty, and it also gives the manufacturer your contact information so they can notify you of product recalls or other important information about your product. However, there's a trick—the form usually includes the basics (your name and address and the product type), but it also often includes a lot of other unnecessary stuff, like questions about your buying preferences and other products you're interested in, for the sole purpose of filling your mailbox with targeted junk mail. Only fill in your name, address, and product identification unless you're specifically required to fill in more to get the warranty, but get that card sent in, as that warranty and other information about the model can be vital.

144. KEEP YOUR WARRANTY AND RECEIPTS

Inevitably, you'll buy an electronic item and it will break. When that happens, it's essential that you have the warranty on hand to know who to contact in order to fix the problem. When you do that, you'll also need to demonstrate when and where you purchased the item. The best way to do that is to keep files on every significant item you buy. Keep a small filing box containing a folder for each major purchase, and within each folder keep the product manual, a copy of the warranty, and the receipt. Whenever you buy a new item, add a new folder to the box with that material inside. That way, when a problem occurs, you'll have all the paperwork you need to take care of the problem in one easy-to-find place.

145. KEEP IT CLEAN AND MINIMIZE THE DUST

One of the biggest dangers to home electronics is dust and dirt. Dust is full of small amounts of metal, and home electronics use metal to store information and transmit data. Thus, it's unsurprising that dust buildup is one of the most common reasons for electronic failure. You can fight that hazard and extend the life of your equipment by keeping it clean and dusting it regularly. If you have a home computer, carefully open the case on occasion and use compressed air to blow out any dust that's built up inside. With other devices, keep the external areas clean and make sure no dust is building up near any ventilation areas, and also make sure the device has plenty of ventilation space (for example, don't move the vents up against a wall). Simple moves like these can vastly extend the life of your home electronics.

146. USE A SURGE PROTECTOR

Most homes receive unexpected electrical surges occasionally, and these surges can damage home electronic devices if the devices are not properly protected. Invest in a surge protector for your most expensive items, preferably one with a switch that you can easily access. This surge protector will prevent your electronics from being damaged during an electrical surge, plus if you have a switch that's accessible, you can utilize it to cut power to all of your electronic devices before you go on a trip, potentially saving you money on energy use as well. A good surge protector is well worth the money. It only takes one prevented surge to make your investment pay off.

147. READ THE MANUAL CAREFULLY, ESPECIALLY ON RECHARGEABLE ITEMS

Whenever you open up a new electronic item, it's well worth the time to give the manual a reading, as there may be less obvious tweaks and settings that can maximize the value and usefulness of the product. Reading the manual is particularly important when it comes to any device that uses an internal rechargeable battery, as such devices often have different optimal ways to charge the battery in order to extend its life. Some devices last longer if completely discharged (used until there is no more juice), while others are better off being charged as often as possible and not allowed to run down to minimal energy. Know what works best for your device and take the steps to ensure a long and healthy lifetime for your new equipment.

148. USE RECHARGEABLE BATTERIES

Rechargeable batteries have come a long way since the nearly unusable battery chargers of a generation ago. Today, top-quality rechargeable batteries, such as the Eneloop batteries available from GE and

Sanyo, don't become weaker after each charge and hold a charge for a very long time, maintaining 85 percent of their charge after a year of sitting on a shelf. An investment in a top-quality battery charger and a sufficient number of rechargeable batteries can keep your home equipped with ample batteries to keep your electronic devices going while saving you significant money over the long haul.

Exchange • Never Be an Early Adopter • Insulate Your Water Heater • Start a Garden • Learn to Love Left-
er • Move to a Cheaper Neighborhood • Rent Out Unused Rooms • Check and Replace Furnace Filters • Dri
Bills on Time • Automate Your Savings • Only Wash Full Loads of Dishes or Clothes • Carpool • Air Up All of

CHEAP TACTIC$ FOR
ENERGY USE

change. • Never Be an Early Adopter • Insulate Your Water Heater • Start a Garden • Learn to Love Leftover
Move to a Cheaper Neighborhood • Rent Out Unused Rooms • Check and Replace Furnace Filters • Drive C
on Time • Automate Your Savings • Only Wash Full Loads of Dishes or Clothes • Carpool • Air Up All of You

149. INSTALL A PROGRAMMABLE THERMOSTAT

A programmable thermostat allows you to automatically raise and lower the temperature in your home at certain times of the day. For example, it can be set to raise the temperature in your house by 10 degrees while you're at work, keeping your air conditioner from running all day, then cooling the house all at once in the early evening just before you arrive home. Instead of just kicking on and off all day, burning energy, your air conditioner would just run for one somewhat longer session in the early evening, saving you significant energy. The reverse would be true with your furnace in cold weather. Your home temperature would automatically drop during the day, warming up again just before you arrive home. You can accomplish this automatically by installing a programmable thermostat in your home, available at your local hardware store for a fairly small price. You can often earn back the cost of the thermostat in just a year due to the energy savings.

150. USE LED BULBS IN CERTAIN PLACES

Compact fluorescent lamp bulbs (CFLs) are currently all the rage for saving energy in your home, but they have their disadvantages—warm-up time, cold light, and cleanup challenges are among the common complaints. LED (light-emitting diode) bulbs, on the other hand, use very little energy and provide directional light (like a flashlight), perfect for lighting needs in small spaces, like closets. One way to get the energy use advantage of CFLs and LEDs without some of the disadvantages is by using a mix of bulbs in your home. Try a three-tiered lighting strategy: normal incandescent for general family areas, CFLs for hall lighting and infrequently used spaces, and LEDs for closet lighting, with a shift toward more LEDs as the technology improves. This will reduce energy use throughout your home and also increase the lifespan of most of your installed bulbs.

151. PUT YOUR HOME ELECTRONICS ON A SWITCH-BASED POWER SOURCE

Many home electronic devices continue to eat electricity even when turned off. The truth is that they often switch into "standby" mode, which means that they slowly consume energy even though they're not in use. Some devices can consume as much as 40 watts in standby mode, which costs you a dime a day at current energy costs. You can solve that problem by putting many of your devices on a single surge protector, then plugging that device into an outlet in your home powered by a switch. When you're done with the equipment, flip the switch. No more lost juice and instant energy savings. Don't have a switch like this? You can get a remote-controlled surge protector that will provide much the same functionality, or other devices that can do the same thing.

152. TURN OFF LIGHTS YOU'RE NOT USING

A typical incandescent bulb uses 60 or 75 watts. That means that every fifteen hours or so, it consumes a kilowatt-hour of energy, costing you a dime at current average energy rates. Going through your home to turn off lights before you leave, or even flipping off switches as you wander through your home, can save significant money over the long haul. Got a strip of lights in your bathroom eating 60 watts each? Leaving them on for just a few hours eats a dime, and flipping off that switch before you leave for work can save you thirty cents or so. A minute's worth of walking through your house to turn off lights can be an extremely cost-effective use of your time.

153. UNPLUG ELECTRICAL DEVICES YOU'RE NOT USING

Don't leave devices that you rarely use plugged in. Many electrical devices use a very small amount of energy from the outlet, called the "phantom load," even when unplugged. Unplug devices like cell phone chargers, laptop chargers, other electronic chargers, and small home electric devices and appliances that you don't use every day, like a toaster. Even with a phantom load of four watts—very common in household devices—you'll end up burning more than a quarter's worth of energy every month (at current energy rates) for each device you leave plugged in without reason. Unplug it and save.

154. PUT ALL DEVICE CHARGERS ON ONE POWER STRIP

Create a power strip that has all of your chargers on it. Get one with a switch at one end for easy convenience. Whenever you need to charge a device, just attach it to the appropriate cord, then flip the switch to turn on the juice; when the device is done, flip the switch to cut the energy. This gives you the convenience of keeping your chargers plugged in and in a standard place along with the energy efficiency of eliminating the phantom power load that slowly adds to your energy bill. You can even get creative and put this strip and charger in a small box with just the switch and the ends of the various chargers exposed. This is an excellent craft project that makes your chargers look a lot neater while also cutting down on your energy use.

155. TURN DOWN YOUR WATER HEATER
The correct temperature setting on your water heater is just hot enough so you can get the heat you actually need when turning on your faucet on full heat. If the water coming out of your faucet is too hot when you've turned it on full blast, turn down your water heater. It'll save you on energy use (and likely save you from a burn from touching water that's too hot). Most water heaters have a very easy temperature adjustment—turn it down a bit and see how things are, then turn it down a bit more if it's still too hot.

156. INSULATE YOUR WATER HEATER
Another useful tactic for reducing energy loss is to insulate your water heater. Many modern water heaters are already well insulated,

but not all are, and even a well-insulated heater can use a little extra help. The Iowa Energy Center reports that a properly installed blanket can reduce energy loss by 25 to 45 percent on a water heater. If you lose even a dollar's worth of energy from your water heater, the blanket will pay for itself in just a few years (and likely you lose even more energy than that). Go to your local hardware store and ask about a water heater blanket.

157. Install Low-Flow Showerheads

The average price of water in the United States is about $1.50 per 1,000 gallons. The national average water flow for showerheads is about 2.6 gallons per minute. You can buy a low-flow showerhead with a switch that reduces the water flow to 1.2 gallons per minute without a noticeable difference in the shower. If you take an average of ten minutes in the shower and you and your spouse take a shower every day, that's 730 showers a year for a total of 7,300 shower-minutes. A low-flow showerhead can save you 1.4 gallons per minute, a total of roughly 10,000 gallons a year. Thus, a low-flow showerhead can save you $15 a year, and modern low-flow showerheads are indistinguishable from normal ones in terms of shower quality.

158. Take Shorter Showers

The average showerhead uses 2.6 gallons of water per minute, and water costs about $1.50 per 1,000 gallons used. If you dawdle in the shower and use five minutes' worth of extra water flow each time you take a daily shower, you waste 4,745 gallons of water each year. That adds up to about $7.50 in lost water for time just spent dawdling when you could be doing something else. Practice taking timed showers. See whether or not you can get in the habit of doing your showering business in just seven minutes, or even just five. Another tactic is to install a showerhead (preferably a low-flow one—see tip #157) with a switch and get in the habit of turning off the water while you lather up, scrub yourself, or put shampoo or conditioner on your hair. If you can stop the water flow for just three minutes while doing these tasks, you save $4.50 a year in water use and help the environment, too.

159. Air-Seal Your Home

Many homes, especially older ones, lose energy to the outdoors almost constantly because of drafts and other air leaks. Blasting cool air outside during the summer, or warm air outside during the winter, can be a significant energy cost. The U.S. Department of Energy states that two simple steps for air-sealing your home, caulking and weather-stripping, will pay for themselves within a year, leaving you with substantial energy savings for years. Visit the Department of Energy's Energy Efficiency and Renewable Energy site to find out more, including a guide to caulking and weather-stripping your home. You can find this information online at *www .eere.energy.gov/consumer*.

160. Adjust Your Home's Temperature Seasonally

Many people find an acceptable temperature in their home and never adjust it again, leaving it at the same temperature year-round. This can eat up significant energy, as your home heating and cooling equipment work year-round to maintain this steady temperature. Instead, adopt a seasonal temperature strategy. If you know what your "standard" temperature is, raise it up 4 degrees in the summer and lower it by 4 degrees in the winter. So, if "normal" is 71 degrees, set it to 75 in the summer and 67 in the winter. This will significantly reduce the effort put forth by your heating and cooling appliances and save you energy money over the long run.

161. Use Heavy Drapes and Blinds

Drapes and blinds serve to minimize the amount of heat transferred through windows by adding an extra layer of insulation. The heavier the drapes and blinds, the better insulation they will provide, thus they'll save you more money on both heating and cooling costs. The larger the window, the more important it is to use heavy drapes and blinds to cover it most of the time, as large windows lose far more energy than small ones.

162. Open and Close the Blinds/Curtains in Tune with the Weather

In the summer, keep the drapes closed, as they'll help block out the sunlight and help keep your home cool. In the winter, keep the drapes closed except when sunlight is directly on the window, then open the drapes and enjoy the "free" heat. In spring and fall, though, when the temperature outside is much the same as it is inside, open up those drapes and open the windows on pleasant days, allowing the air to flow in and out freely. Doing this habitually can save a lot of money on your energy bill, as it allows you to take advantage of external heat when it's beneficial and block it when it's a hindrance.

163. Use the "Hibernate" Mode on Your Computer

"Hibernation" mode, if available on your computer, is the best possible balance of intelligent energy use and convenience in powering up. Putting your computer in "hibernate" means that it copies your current computer state to the hard drive, then powers down the computer entirely, just as if you had turned it off. When you power up again, though, the computer reads the stored state and returns your computer to the exact same situation that it was in before you put it in hibernate mode. Many people do not like the inconvenience of going through a computer's lengthy start-up. "Hibernate" mode allows you to take advantage of the huge energy savings from powering down your computer when you're not using it coupled with most of the convenience of a quick start-up.

164. Close Off Unused Rooms

If there are rooms in your house that are rarely used, close them off so that you're not wasting energy heating and cooling those rooms.

Pull the blinds tight, close any vents in the room, and then close the door tightly, even stuffing any significant gaps under the door. This room will typically be warmer than the rest of the house in summer and cooler than the rest in winter due to the reduced energy used to heat and cool that room, and that reduced use goes straight into your pocket in the form of a smaller energy bill.

165. Clean Out Your Air Vents

Over time, the air vents in your home will slowly get clogged with dust, especially dust that's not visible at a glance. Once every year or two, spend the time to take a duster to every vent in your home, remove the cover, and dust deeply inside the vent to make sure there's no dust building up in there. Also, ensure that none of the vents in your home are covered up or obstructed—for instance, by a chair or bed—as blocked vents are incredibly inefficient. Rearranging a room to unblock a vent is well worth the effort in terms of money saved.

166. Install Ceiling Fans in Every Room You Spend Time In

Ceiling fans are brilliant tools for reducing energy use in every season, but you have to be a bit clever to maximize their value. In the winter, set the fan to run in a clockwise direction, which pulls the warm air from the ceiling and pushes it down toward the floor, subtly raising the temperature in the room and causing the heating system to work less. In the summer, have the fan run in the opposite direction, which maximizes the circulation benefit of a fan. Air circulation can make the room feel as much as 8 degrees cooler, and combined with a temperature-adjustment strategy it can save you as much as 30 percent on your cooling bill.

167. Do an Insulation Inspection

Unsurprisingly, having good insulation in the attic can make a huge difference in the amount of energy you expend in the winter keeping your home warm. In most modern homes, it's easy to check this. The attic is mostly loaded with insulation on the floor, so take a peek up there and see what you notice. Are there any bare areas? That's going to be a heat leak, so make sure you have insulation placed in that area. Also, if you're able to, note the resistance rating of the insulation in your attic. It's usually noted with the letter R followed by a number. Ideally, you want insulation between R-21 and R-30. If it's low, like R-10, you should consider installing some higher-resistance insulation on top of the existing insulation without pressing down the existing insulation. Your local hardware store will be glad to offer advice and suggestions.

168. Do Proper Maintenance on Your Furnace and Air-Conditioning Unit

Home energy use often revolves around your furnace and your air-conditioning unit, which is why so many of these tips focus on improving their efficiency. Efficiency doesn't matter, though, if your units aren't functioning well, and the best way to maintain their functionality is by performing regular maintenance on the devices. Make sure their vents are clean. Replace the filters in your air-handling system regularly. Make absolutely sure that you haven't stacked anything on or around your outside air-conditioning unit. These little tips will go a long way toward keeping your heating and cooling units running efficiently, and might even extend their life, putting money right in your pocket.

169. PLANT SHADE TREES

Planting shade trees on your property not only increases property value, but a well-placed shade tree can block direct sunlight from hitting your house, providing a direct reduction in the amount of energy you'll need to use to keep your home cool. Find a fast-growing tree that can provide ample shade for your home in your climate and plant it to the east or to the west of your home. Not only does a shade tree add property value and reduce energy use, but it also provides enjoyment for the family, like a great place to lounge on a lazy day.

Change • Never Be an Early Adopter • Insulate Your Water Heater • Start a Garden • Learn to Love Leftovers
Move to a Cheaper Neighborhood • Rent Out Unused Rooms • Check and Replace Furnace Filters • Drive Ca
in Tune • Automate Your Savings • Only Wash Full Loads of Dishes or Clothes • Carpool • Air Up All of Your

CHEAP TACTIC$ FOR
FUN AND HOBBIES

170. CUT BACK ON HOBBIES THAT CONSTANTLY REQUIRE BUYING MORE STUFF

Hobbies that require a constant influx of money—golf, for example—are dangerous to your financial well-being. In order to enjoy the game, you have to pay for greens fees, cart rentals, balls, clubs, and so forth, and playing regularly can become a serious drain on your money. Many collections are the same way. In order to increase the size of your collection, you often have to spend additional money. Cut back on these hobbies, which require constant money and resources, and instead find other hobbies that don't require that money influx.

171. CHECK THE COMMUNITY CALENDAR

If you're looking for free or low-cost entertainment in your community, look for a community calendar that provides a listing of all of these events. You might have to do a little footwork to track one down. Try visiting city hall, the chamber of commerce, the visitor's center, the library, or the post office, or visiting the city's website. They will list lots of free activities going on in your town, many of which you likely aren't aware of. If you start choosing an evening activity or two a week from the community calendar, that's time you're not out and about spending money.

172. Visit the Post Office

Most communities have a vibrant community bulletin board at the local post office. Stop in and see what's on the board. You'll often see notices of interesting community events, notices of people selling items extremely cheaply (many times just before a move), new local businesses and organizations, job opportunities, and countless other items of interest. Whenever you're in your local post office mailing a package, it's worth your time to take a serious look at the bulletin board. You might just save yourself some money or find something useful for cheap.

173. Read the Local Newspaper

Another venue for finding out about local activities and organizations is the community newspaper. Newspapers often include announcements of upcoming events, descriptions of the activities of local organizations, and countless other little things that you can use to get involved in your community. Even better, many alternative local newspapers are free on the newsstand. Check near the entrances of community centers and local grocery stores for a free copy. These papers are a treasure trove of engaging and interesting activities of all kinds that won't pinch your wallet.

174. Stop By Your Town's Visitor's Center

Towns and cities often have an interesting cultural or historical heritage that many residents are only remotely aware of. Spend a few minutes at your town's visitor's center to find out about these interesting local resources, and spend an afternoon or two visiting them. You might be surprised at the genuinely interesting and engaging historical and cultural elements around you. Many of them can be enjoyed without spending any money at all.

175. CHECK OUT THE LIBRARY—NOT JUST FOR BOOKS

The local library has become an absolute treasure trove of entertainment options. Beyond the enormous collection of books, most local libraries have extensive CD and DVD collections that can be checked out for free or at low cost, and many have extensive magazine collections so you can catch up on your interests. Many community libraries also have movie nights, where you can watch a film in a theater setting for free. Libraries are also often hubs for all sorts of special-interest groups, from gardeners to people who enjoy playing bridge. In many communities, libraries are also a source of free Internet access. Most communities give out a free library card to anyone who lives in the community and often give free memberships to anyone living in adjacent cities and towns as well. Take the time to visit your local library. You might be genuinely surprised at all they have to offer.

176. HAVE A MONEY-FREE WEEKEND

Transform the idea of living cheap into something fun. Challenge yourself and your friends to spend this entire weekend without spending any money. Look for free activities to do as a group. Eat using the stuff you already have in the cupboards. Engage in personal activities that don't require you to spend money, like curling up with that book you've had for a while that you've been intending to read or going through the junk in the downstairs closet. Get into a routine of having money-free weekends once a month, or even once every other weekend, and you'll find your entertainment expenses (and expenses in other areas) will go down rapidly.

177. SEE WHAT YOUR LOCAL COLLEGE OR UNIVERSITY HAS TO OFFER

If you live near a local college or university, particularly a large one, there's almost constantly a string of interesting speakers and activities happening on campus. Visit the school's website (or call their general information number) and find out what's on tap in the near future, then attend a meeting or a lecture on a topic that's compelling to you. Many student organizations are open to the community at large and often welcome people who are not students to participate, so if there's a group focusing on an area of interest to you, don't be afraid to dive in and get involved.

178. START A NATURAL COLLECTION

If you enjoy collecting things but are finding that your collections are costing you a lot of money, start a new type of collection. Spend your time collecting things that can be found in nature, like rocks of a particular color or type, leaves of particular trees, or pictures of birds. Think about what interests you, then look around in your natural environment for examples that you can collect.

179. DIG THROUGH YOUR MEDIA COLLECTION

Many people have extensive collections of books, magazines, DVDs, CDs, and so forth. You can utilize these resources to earn some extra money, but you can also use them for a great deal of entertainment as well. Whenever you find yourself bored and itching for entertainment, go through your collection and pull out a few items that you may have forgotten about and dig in. Usually, you'll find an item or two that, when you see it, will make you feel a bit excited and think, "I'd forgotten all about that! Cool!" When you have that feeling, you have instant entertainment in your hands without any cost at all—a great way to save money on entertainment.

180. SHOP FOR USED DVDs, CDs, AND BOOKS

When you decide to make an addition to your DVD, CD, book, or video game collection, start by looking in the used stores—particularly if what you're looking for is not the latest release. If you can find the item you're seeking in a used form, you'll save yourself money versus buying it new. Even better, if you're browsing for inspiration, start off browsing in the used section so that if you do find something, it won't cost you nearly as much. Used selections often include items that you'll have a difficult time finding new, such as

---

out-of-print books and obscure CDs and DVDs. Start there, and you might find a cheap gem.

181. Swap Your Used DVDs, CDs, and Books Online

One way to keep yourself awash with fresh material to read, watch, or listen to is to participate in online clubs for swapping these items. PaperBackSwap (*www.paperbackswap.com*) is an excellent resource for swapping books. Just list the books you're willing to trade on the site and when someone requests the book, you send it out and earn a credit. You can then spend that credit on the site to have a book shipped to you. Swap-A-CD (*www.swapacd.com*) and Swap-A-DVD (*www.swapadvd.com*) offer very similar services online for CDs and DVDs. It's a great way to give yourself something fresh to listen to, watch, or read on a regular basis without leaving the comfort of your home.

182. Play Games for Free Online

If you enjoy playing classic games like chess, checkers, bridge, canasta, and so forth, there are many places where you can play the games for free against an opponent in another town over the Internet. Just sign up at Yahoo! Games (*http://games.yahoo.com*), make up a username, and join the game. The site offers a wide array of games that you can play against online opponents for free. If you like playing video games, try Kongregate (*www.kongregate.com*), where you can sign up and play a huge variety of games of all kinds, from puzzle games to action games and strategy games. These games cost you nothing and can provide nearly endless hours of entertainment if you have a home PC with Internet access.

183. LEARN A NEW CARD GAME

Card games are another incredibly inexpensive way to enjoy an evening with friends or a rainy afternoon at the kitchen table. Spend some time to learn a new game, or call some friends and invite them over for an evening of playing an old familiar card game. In either case, you've got hours of fun, social entertainment for just the cost of a pack of cards. Cards can also be a social opportunity to meet new people. See if your community has a bridge, canasta, or pinochle club. Such clubs can be a very inexpensive way to meet new people, have a great deal of fun, and stretch your mind a bit, too.

184. TEACH YOURSELF A SKILL YOU'VE ALWAYS WANTED TO LEARN

A lazy afternoon is a perfect time to teach yourself a new skill. Why not spend an hour learning how to knit a scarf? Perhaps you can spend an afternoon learning how to play that musical instrument in your closet, or maybe you've always wanted to tackle making an egg soufflé. Don't put such ideas off. Learning a new skill, especially with friends, can be fun, and many skills can also end up saving you a lot of money over the long run.

185. Go Exploring

Another great way to spend time without spending money is to go exploring, even in your own neighborhood. Visit areas that you've never been to before, just to see what sorts of interesting things are there. This can be a great family activity. Take a "wandering walk" in your neighborhood by merely going out your front door and going in whichever direction looks the most interesting. Alternately, visit the nearest state park and spend some time exploring the wonderful outdoors, going on trails, and admiring the beauty of nature.

186. Read More

Reading is perhaps the cheapest hobby you can have. The library provides a nearly infinite supply of reading materials for free, plus the time invested in reading costs only as much as the energy cost of the light bulb over your head (or nothing at all, if you read outside). Even if you've never read much before in your life, try picking up a book that looks interesting and start digging in. You might surprise yourself and find something truly compelling. If you already read regularly, try trimming some time away from other expensive hobbies and devote a bit more time to reading. It's a healthy and mentally invigorating hobby.

187. Watch Less Television

According to the South Dakota Department of Health, the average adult watches television for 31.5 hours a week. That's a lot of time lost, but it's also expensive; the average cable/satellite bill runs around $50 a month. That's not all. The average television uses about 75 watts of energy and the average cable box uses 15 watts. That means in an average year, television usage eats up $15 worth of energy, too. And we're not even including the cost of buying the television. Even more problematic is that television is laden with commercials encouraging you to buy more stuff, both during the commercial breaks and via product placements in the programs themselves. Do yourself a favor and cut back on television viewing. You'll not only cut back on your energy use (saving money), but you'll also find yourself having more time to do the things you wish you had time to do, like talking to a relative or an old friend or taking care of an unfinished household task. Turn the television off and you'll have time to turn some of your life back on.

change • Never Be an Early Adopter • Insulate Your Water Heater • Start a Garden • Learn to Love Leftovers
Move to a Cheaper Neighborhood • Rent Out Unused Rooms • Check and Replace Furnace Filters • Drive Ca
on Time • Automate Your Savings • Only Wash Full Loads of Dishes or Clothes • Carpool • Air Up All of Your

CHEAP TACTIC$ FOR

GROCERIES AND SUPPLIES

g exchange • Never Be an Early Adopter • Insulate Your Water Heater • Start a Garden • Learn to Love Left
ter • Move to a Cheaper Neighborhood • Rent Out Unused Rooms • Check and Replace Furnace Filters • Dr
Bills on Time • Automate Your Savings • Only Wash Full Loads of Dishes or Clothes • Carpool • Air Up All o

188. Don't Eat Out as Often

Eating out on a regular basis can get very expensive. Aside from low-end fast food, there's almost no meal you can eat outside the home that's not far more expensive than a virtually identical dish you can prepare at home. You can usually prepare it much faster and with healthier ingredients. The only way to get good at this, and to really reap the cost benefits of eating at home, is to do it all the time. Reduce eating out (and ordering delivery or take-out) to special occasions only and start busting out the pots and pans more often. Not only will your wallet thank you, but your taste buds will, too. As you gain more practice at cooking, your dishes will become more delicious.

189. Go Grocery Shopping Once a Week at Most

Think about your average grocery store trip. You wind up buying mostly stuff you need, but a few odd and unexpected items always wind up in your cart. You've usually got enough fortitude to keep the items to a minimum, but they wind up in there each trip. The simplest way to curtail those extra items, and to save on gas and time as well, is to get into a routine of going to the grocery store less often. You should go once a week at most. Not only will you save time and gas this way, but you'll also cut down on the number of extras you dump into the cart.

190. Eat Before You Go Grocery Shopping

One of the most dangerous expenses in the grocery store is the impulse buy, and impulse buys are often directly caused by hunger. When you're in a grocery store and you're feeling hungry, many more items are going to look tasty to you and are thus much more likely to sneak their way into your cart. There's a simple way to suppress this grocery shopping impulse: Eat a small meal just before you leave to go grocery shopping. That way you're not hungry, but you're also not bogged down with a heavy meal in your stomach. This will allow you to keep your energy up and get finished with shopping quickly, but not be tempted to throw extras into your cart just because you're hungry and impulsive.

191. Plan Your Meals Using the Grocery Store Flyer

Another effective way to manage those weekly grocery store trips is to start off with a plan for what you'll eat in the coming week. The cheapest way to get started is to pull out the flyer from your local grocery store (often included in community flyers or in the Sunday paper) and see which items are being sold very cheaply to get you in the door. Identify a handful of these, then use them to plan your meals for the week by using those items as the core ingredients in most if not all of your dishes. For example, if you notice that chicken is discounted highly, as is broccoli, look for dishes that utilize both and plan one or two of them for the week. Not only does this reduce your cost, but it also encourages diverse meals when you base your meals on what's on sale instead of eating the same old tired thing you buy on every grocery trip.

192. Make a Grocery List Before You Go

Once you have the meal plan ready, make a list of all of the ingredients you'll need for those dishes that you don't have on hand and any other staples you might need in a pinch. Take this to the store with you and use it. That means focus on nothing but gathering the items on the list and getting them into the cart. With a focused list like this, you know everything you need is on the list, thus you don't have to wander down the aisles or through the produce section hoping to stumble upon an idea for a meal to prepare. Everything you need is on that list. This not only saves you time in the store, but it also greatly reduces impulse buying.

193. Get Comfortable with Cooking

One major challenge that keeps many people out of the kitchen is a fear of cooking. The easiest way to get comfortable with cooking is just to try it, starting with simple recipes. You don't have to match the latest amazing creation you saw on television. Just try beating some eggs and a dash of milk with a spoon and cooking it in a pan over medium heat, scraping the eggs away from the side until it tastes right. With only ten minutes, three eggs, and a pinch of salt, you have a delicious meal for just thirty cents or so. When you start with simple recipes and do them over and over again, you start mastering the little techniques, and eventually the things that seemed impossible before may not seem so hard—eventually they may even seem easy. The biggest step, though, is the first one. Get out there in your kitchen and try something.

194. AVOID FROZEN AND PREPACKAGED MEALS

On the surface, these seem like good deals—complete meals for just a few dollars! But once you read the ingredient list, then open up the package and see what you actually get for your dollar, it becomes a pretty poor deal, indeed. You should cut frozen and prepackaged meals out of your buying habits. If you like the convenience of just pulling a meal out of the freezer, popping it in the microwave, and chowing down, prepare a bunch of individual frozen meals in advance, like handmade frozen burritos and the like. Your cost per item will drop and the food will be healthier, too.

195. MAKE RECIPES WITH INEXPENSIVE BASE INGREDIENTS

One quick way to start saving serious money in the kitchen is by learning how to cook inexpensive staple foods very well. Learn the art of preparing beans and bean dishes, for starters, and focus on other inexpensive staple foods: fresh vegetables and fruit in season, eggs, pasta, tuna, and oatmeal are all inexpensive places to start. Coupled with a strong assortment of basic spices, you have the backbone of many wonderful meals just with those basic items in various combinations—fresh fruit in oatmeal, pasta with tuna, pasta with tuna and fresh vegetables, beans with fresh vegetables, beans with eggs, and so on. If you learn to master these basic staples in the kitchen, it'll be much easier to move on to more advanced recipes—and you'll save a ton of money as you learn.

196. Start a Garden

If you have a bit of space where you live to break ground, gardening can be an extremely cost-effective hobby and can be as good as putting money in your pocket. You have to make some up-front investments—the cost of seeds and starter plants, the cost of a hoe or other equipment to break ground, and the time investment needed to tend to your plants—but you'll earn a nice harvest at the end of the summer. You'll have spent a lot of time in the garden on a very frugal activity, time you might have spent elsewhere engaging in expensive hobbies. In some fruitful seasons, you'll more than break even with the value of the produce you grow, and you have the freedom to grow the foods that you like. Don't have space? Try starting a window garden or a box garden. You can grow a small amount of food in one of these in even the tightest of spaces.

197. Learn to Love Leftovers

Many people turn up their nose at the idea of leftovers. The mere thought of reheating food originally prepared a day or two before convinces many that the food will be bland and rubbery, not worth eating. This assumption sadly results in a lot of good, quality food hitting the trash can before its time. The truth is that with a little bit of careful planning, leftovers can be a delicious and highly inexpensive meal. Some ideas:

► Add additional spices that you have on hand to leftovers just before you serve them. This will create a fresh snap to the flavor of the food.
► Use the leftovers as the basis for a second meal. For example, take leftover spaghetti and sauce, chop up the spaghetti, put it in a bread loaf pan, sprinkle some mozzarella cheese on the top, and bake it in the oven. Or take the leftover chicken breasts from the grill, dice them, and add them to a rice and vegetable skillet meal.
► Freeze the leftovers. This especially works well if you've made a large batch of soup and have plenty left over. Freeze it in portion-sized containers.

198. Buy Staples in Bulk

Buying in bulk can save you a great deal of money, but not if you wind up wasting part of your purchase by letting it grow old before you use it. Focus on buying only nonperishables and key staple foods that you use all the time in bulk. If you use a bulk purchase in its entirety, you'll almost always save money.

199. Freeze Extra Staple Foods

Another tactic for effectively using freezer space, especially if you have a deep freezer, is to freeze any extra staple foods you are able to purchase or make. For example, loaves of bread can be frozen and kept fresh for a short while, as can many fresh vegetables. This isn't a long-term solution for food storage as freezer burn can be an issue, but if you hit upon a big bargain on fresh vegetables, don't be afraid to take advantage of the sale and stock up, freezing the excess in portion-sized bags to thaw and use later on.

200. Cook in Advance and Freeze Complete Meals

Many busy families resort to eating out regularly simply because of time constraints, even though this maneuver costs them considerable money over the long haul. A much more sensible tactic is to prepare complete meals in advance and freeze them so that when the time comes to use the meals, they can be pulled out of the freezer and tossed into the oven. Spending time preparing meals to be frozen in advance is a great way to spend one day every month or two, especially when the cost savings of eating such prepared meals adds up so quickly when home-cooked meals replace those eaten out.

201. Prepare Extra Batches of Other Meals

Preparing a casserole for supper? Why not simultaneously prepare two or three casseroles, then pop the extras in the freezer for future use? This not only saves you a great deal of time later, but it actually saves you money now because it allows you to buy the ingredients of meals in bulk and use them immediately. For example, preparing three identical tuna noodle casseroles instead of one takes a bit of extra time up-front, but it saves a huge amount of time later on as you can just pull one out of the freezer. Better yet, because you're making so much at once, you can buy the large bags of noodles and the large cans of tuna, reducing the cost of each casserole by a noticeable amount.

202. MASTER THE ART OF THE SLOW COOKER

The slow cooker often creates visions in people's heads of mushy, tired, and bland food, not interesting to eat at all. That's a stereotype that's quickly being relegated to the dustbin of history, as modern slow cookers with timers are able to turn on when you want them to, creating perfectly cooked meals that finish exactly when you've specified. A slow cooker is a perfect way to cook a stew, a soup, a casserole, or a large cut of meat while you're at work, allowing you to walk in the door to a perfectly prepared meal. The slow cooker can be a massive time-saver, allowing you to eat at home on a highly pinched schedule and thus enjoy the cost savings of eating at home with the in-a-pinch convenience of eating out. Dig out your slow cooker and try some recipes—you'll be pleasantly surprised. Don't have a timer? Stop by your local hardware store and ask about an outlet timer, a device that plugs into an electrical outlet and only turns on power at a specified time. This can allow your slow cooker to turn on a few hours before you get home, creating a perfectly cooked meal just as you walk in the door.

203. Cut Down on Coffee, Soft Drinks, and Bottled Water

Not only are drinks such as soda and coffee generally unhealthy for you (creating a caffeine addiction and often loading your body with sugars and high fructose corn syrup), they're also far more expensive than water. Even if you spend as little as $1 on average per day brewing your own coffee, that adds up to $365 a year; a daily Starbucks habit can easily add up to $1,700 a year. Try replacing parts of your beverage diet with cool, clean tap water (or filtered water). Bottled water, on the other hand, is just a way to pay a significant premium for convenience. Get a refillable and reliable set of plastic water bottles and keep them filled in the refrigerator yourself from your own tap. If you prefer filtered water, you're still saving big money—most filtered water units pay for themselves in just a few weeks as compared to the cost of bottled water. Eliminating just a few beverages a day can easily save you $100 a year and help you live healthier, too.

204. Look into Joining a Community-Supported Agriculture Group

A community-supported agriculture group is a system in which a number of customers who use lots of fresh produce get together to financially support a farmer to grow vegetables and fruits for them.

You can think of it as a large number of households getting together to mutually hire a fruit and vegetable gardener. The typical cost of a CSA is $300 to $500 a share for eighteen to twenty weeks, and the food produced for a share is enough to handle the vegetable and fruit needs for two people. In other words, you pay roughly $20 a week in advance to get fresh produce delivered to you each week for most of the summer and early fall. If your diet is already heavy in fresh produce, a CSA effectively functions as bulk buying of vegetables. They're substantially cheaper than buying the same quantity of fruits and vegetables at the store, plus the produce is much, much fresher as it's grown locally and is usually just a day or two from being in the ground when it arrives at your door. If you eat a lot of fresh produce, a CSA can be a tremendous bargain.

205. Shop at a Farmers' Market

Many communities hold a weekly farmers' market where individual producers of vegetables, fruits, and other goods go to ply their wares. Often the prices are reasonable and comparable to the prices you'd pay at the grocery store, plus the produce is fresher and you have an opportunity to talk with the producers to find out suggestions for preparing the food and so on. A good food preparation idea can be more valuable than the food itself. *Another tip:* Try shopping late in the session, when farmers often cut their prices to get rid of unwanted produce. Although you may have to pick through some of the lesser produce you can get a substantial bargain at the end of a farmers' market.

206. Buy Generic Brand Products

Generic and store-brand products are often shunned by shoppers simply because of the unfamiliar label. It's often "safer" to buy a name brand than the generic. This line of thinking is nonsense. Often, the generic version is identical to the name brand except for the label and the sticker price. Not sure? If you discover that it's not up to your standards, switch back to the name brand. You'll likely be surprised, though, not just by the level of quality, but by the money you save in buying generics.

207. Try a More Value-Oriented Grocery Store

Most areas have a number of grocery stores that serve different levels of buyers. Some, like Whole Foods, cater to high-end buyers who are willing to spend more for organics and other such items. At the other end of the spectrum are grocery stores focused on economical foods. These stores usually use minimal advertising and find other ways to reduce costs for the customer. Give one of these value-oriented grocery stores a try. You might be pleasantly surprised to find that you can buy the exact same items at the value-oriented store as at the other stores, except significantly cheaper.

208. Master the Concept of Cost per Use

Cost per use is a tremendously useful way to compare all sorts of different items that you might buy, from breakfast cereals to shoes. The cost per use of an item is the cost of the item divided by the number of times you'll use it before it wears out, and the lower the cost per use of the item, the better value it is and the more money you'll save by buying it. Take, for example, two pairs of shoes. One costs $50 but is guaranteed to stand up to three years of wear. Another pair is $10 and will likely last only six months or so as it is cheaply made. The $10 pair might seem like the better deal, but the cost per use of the $50 shoes is significantly lower. For each month of use, you'll save twenty-eight cents automatically with the $50 shoes. In other words, it's often more cost-effective, and thus cheaper over the long haul, to buy the more expensive version that's guaranteed to last longer. You can apply this principle to virtually anything you might buy, from washing machines to toothpaste, and the principle holds up. The cheaper you can get the cost per use to be, the cheaper the item is overall, regardless of the sticker price. Give it some practice and you'll be surprised how quite often expensive things are actually cheap and cheap things are actually expensive.

209. GET MAXIMUM USE OUT OF SUPPLIES LIKE BAKING SODA AND VINEGAR

Baking soda, vinegar, and water are pretty much all you need for most cleaning situations in your home, and considering you can buy these items cheaply at the grocery store, consider switching to them for your cleaning needs. Need to scrub something down? Make a paste out of a spoonful of baking soda and a spoonful of water and use that paste to scrub the dirty dish or spot on the floor. Want to mop? Dilute a few capfuls of vinegar in a bucket of water and use that to mop things down. Got some foul odors? Sprinkle some baking soda on the source of the stench, or dilute some vinegar in water and use a spray bottle to spray a mist around the room. Got greasy dishes? Use some vinegar with the hot water to cut right through the grease. Baking soda and vinegar alone can take care of the chores you might have originally used a large array of unnecessarily expensive items for. Want more ideas? Search online for "baking soda uses" or "vinegar uses" for many more tips.

g Exchange • Never Be an Early Adopter • Insulate Your Water Heater • Start a Garden • Learn to Love Left
er • Move to a Cheaper Neighborhood • Rent Out Unused Rooms • Check and Replace Furnace Filters • Dri
Bills on Time • Automate Your Savings • Only Wash Full Loads of Dishes or Clothes • Carpool • Air Up All of

CHEAP TACTIC$ FOR
HEALTH

210. Exercise Regularly

Over the long term, regular exercise is one of the most cost-effective ways around to live cheap. Exercise can be very inexpensive, lifts your energy level (improving your earning potential), and improves your long-term health (reducing health care costs). Consult your doctor and begin a simple exercise plan. No matter what shape you're in, a bit of exercise can do a great deal of good for you now and for your long-term health as well.

211. Find an Exercise Buddy or Two

With a packed schedule and many distractions, it's very easy to simply not exercise. Turn both of those around by finding an exercise buddy or two, people with whom you feel comfortable exercising multiple times a week. Use exercising as a social occasion and motivate each other to get into better shape. A morning walk or jog with a friend or a half hour after work playing basketball with some buddies can make it much easier and more enjoyable to actually get in better shape.

212. Slowly Substitute Healthier Food Options

Another cheap way to better health is to improve your diet, but as with anything, it's often hard to make a radical change to your diet and stick with it. Instead, improve your diet by slowly substituting inexpensive but healthy food options for unhealthy items. For example, choose to order a salad instead of an entrée at a restaurant. Not only will it be less expensive, but it'll be healthier, too. Try slowly substituting water for coffee and soda. It's less expensive and substantially healthier. Swap out your ice cream for some frozen yogurt or try making it yourself.

213. EAT A BALANCED DIET

Another effective way to manipulate your food consumption to save money over the long haul is to keep it balanced. Make vegetables and fruit the largest portion of your diet, but keep it varied. Focus your food spending on whatever produce is on sale that week, then get something completely different that's on sale the next week. This keeps your diet varied, balanced, and inexpensive, resulting in better health over the long run.

214. USE YOUR FLEXIBLE SPENDING ACCOUNT

Many employers offer a flexible spending account to accompany their health insurance plan. This flexible spending account allows you to pay for some medical expenses with pre-tax money, saving you on your income tax. Take advantage of this if it's available to you, particularly if you have any maintenance prescriptions, ongoing health situations, or dependents who may have medical concerns. In fact, your flexible spending account can make it cheaper to go to your own regular medical checkups, which will go a long way toward keeping you in good health.

215. WASH YOUR HANDS

The common cold destroys countless hours of productivity each year, causing people to miss days at work and miss out on income and other opportunities as well. If you're self-employed, a cold can be utterly devastating, resulting in lost work hours, missed contract opportunities, and other negative effects. These lost opportunities can often be prevented by doing the simplest of things to prevent the common cold: washing your hands regularly. Wash them every time you use the restroom and just before you handle food. Doing both will go a long way toward reducing your chances of getting a devastating cold.

216. PRACTICE GOOD HYGIENE

Along with washing your hands, you can not only prevent illnesses but also improve your appearance to others by practicing good basic hygiene. For many, this is common sense, but it only takes one whiff of a person with bad breath to see how devastating that poor hygiene can be and one look at a person with bad teeth to see how costly poor hygiene can be. Take a shower daily. Brush your teeth at least once a day. Use deodorant. Keep your clothes clean. The key is to keep yourself presentable and avoid germs that could bring on illness.

217. DRINK MORE WATER

Drinking adequate amounts of water improves your energy, increases your mental and physical performance, removes toxins from your body, reduces the chances of a heart attack, and helps you lose weight. Pretty amazing what a few more glasses of water can do each day, isn't it? The average American drinks far less than the appropriate amount of water each day. You should be drinking eight 8-ounce cups of water each day at a minimum (approximately five tumbler glasses full of water). Not drinking that much? Try drinking a tumbler full of water each time you begin to feel hungry during the day, making sure that you drink your minimum of five a day. You'll find your hunger lessens (saving you money on food) and after a while you'll begin to feel genuinely better both physically and mentally (improving your earning potential). That's not even counting the other health benefits. A glass of water is the best cheapskate deal of all.

218. Eat Breakfast Every Day

Eating a low-fat breakfast each morning, such as a bowl of healthy cereal or a piece of fruit, not only has a tremendous positive effect on your late-morning energy level and mood, but it also improves mental performance throughout the day. Even better, it keeps you thin by getting your metabolism going earlier in the day. Not only that, it also has the effect of subtly reducing your appetite at lunchtime and later in the day, resulting in lower overall food costs if you eat an inexpensive breakfast. A quick banana on your way to work can end up making your workday easier and save you money on lower food costs over the long run.

219. ELIMINATE SMOKING AND MINIMIZE DRINKING

Drinking and smoking, especially when done with any frequency, can be incredibly expensive habits by themselves, never mind the high health care costs they can bring on later in life. If you're a regular user of either, work hard to break the habit and you'll find yourself with substantially more money in your pocket and better all-around health, both now and in the future. If you're having trouble breaking the habit, ask for help from your friends and family. They'll help you work through breaking a difficult habit.

220. SLEEP MORE

Sleeping more by itself doesn't directly save you money, but inadequate sleep can certainly cost you money. Lack of sleep can reduce your mental sharpness, costing you money when you make silly mistakes. It can also cause you to spend money on convenience because you're tired, and it can also make you more susceptible to advertising and coercion because your mental defenses aren't sharp. Make sure you get an adequate amount of sleep each night, seven to eight hours at least, to ensure that your mind is sharp and you don't lose money in such preventable ways.

221. SCHEDULE REGULAR MEDICAL AND DENTAL CHECKUPS

Many medical and dental conditions can be easily and inexpensively treated if caught in the early stages, but can be very expensive to deal with if caught in later stages. The solution to this conundrum is simple: Get regular medical and dental checkups. Such regular checkups are covered by almost all health insurance policies, as it's far cheaper for the insurance companies, too. So regular checkups often incur only the smallest of expenses while avoiding some potentially monstrous expenses down the road. Regular medical and dental checkups are an incredibly cheap deal compared to the huge costs you might face without them.

222. Talk to Your Doctor about Independent Steps

If you discover that you have a medical condition, ask your doctor about independent steps you can take to minimize the effects no matter what the condition is. Almost every condition can be improved by making certain choices in your life, and making those choices can almost always reduce your potential future medical bills. So, if you're diagnosed with a condition, always ask what you can do to help minimize the effects or damage of that condition.

223. Consider Traveling for Surgeries or Other Medical Care

One medical option that many people don't consider is the possibility of traveling to another country for expensive medical care, such as major surgeries or lengthy treatments. Depending on your insurance, you may be able to save a significant amount of money out of your own pocket by exploring these opportunities. If it appears as though a surgery or other major medical procedure is in your future, call your health insurer and ask if there are any available options for reducing the overall cost, including traveling to another region of the country or traveling abroad for the procedure. Many insurance companies are quite happy to send you to another country for medical work, then send you back, in order to save a significant amount on the procedure, as it can be done in other areas at the same level of quality for much less. If you find out that you are going to have a major medical procedure, don't panic. A bit of planning now can save you a ton of money later.

224. Ask Your Doctor for Prescription Samples

Whenever you're given a prescription, ask your doctor if they have any samples of the prescription available that they can give you. In many cases, the sample may be enough to eliminate a prescription refill, saving you money. It can also tide you over until you can go to a lower-cost pharmacy to get your prescription filled, saving you money merely by giving you more freedom to choose your pharmacy.

225. Ask Your Doctor about Generics

Now that many pharmacies are offering $4 generic prescriptions, you can save quite a bit of money merely by asking your doctor whether or not there is a generic version of your prescription available that will work for your condition. In many cases, the generic is a perfect equivalent of the name-brand prescription, and thus substituting the generic for the name-brand prescription can save you a great deal of money at the pharmacy. Always ask your doctor about generics when you're given a prescription. It can save you a lot of money, particularly on a maintenance prescription that you'll refill many times.

change • Never Be an Early Adopter • Insulate Your Water Heater • Start a Garden • Learn to Love Leftovers
Move to a Cheaper Neighborhood • Rent Out Unused Rooms • Check and Replace Furnace Filters • Drive Ca
on Time • Automate Your Savings • Only Wash Full Loads of Dishes or Clothes • Carpool • Air Up All of Your

CHEAP TACTIC$ FOR
HOUSING

ng Exchange • Never Be an Early Adopter • Insulate Your Water Heater • Start a Garden • Learn to Love Left-
ter • Move to a Cheaper Neighborhood • Rent Out Unused Rooms • Check and Replace Furnace Filters • Or
Bills on Time • Automate Your Savings • Only Wash Full Loads of Dishes or Clothes • Carpool • Air Up All o

226. IF YOU'RE PLANNING ON MOVING IN THE NEXT FIVE YEARS, RENT

Considering buying a home because it's a "good investment"? That idea is conventional wisdom, but there are many cases where it simply isn't true. For example, if you're intending to move away from the area within the next five years, it's more cost-effective to rent rather than buy. Why? During the first five years of your mortgage, almost all of your payment will go toward interest in the property, not toward equity. In fact, when you consider the closing costs from buying the house, plus the realtor fees when you sell the house, that will eat all of the equity in the house and more in almost all housing markets. Instead, look for an inexpensive place to rent in the area until you're ready to move on, as rent is almost always far cheaper than house payments. Sock away that difference for the future.

227. IF YOU DON'T HAVE A DOWN PAYMENT YET, RENT

It's tempting to go ahead and buy a home as soon as you feel ready, regardless of whether you have the money or not. However, diving into buying a home without a full down payment can be a huge financial mistake that will cost you for decades. Most lenders expect you to have 20 percent down when you buy a home. Buying without that down payment usually gives you several options, none of them pretty: a second, smaller loan with a much higher interest rate, or private mortgage insurance to ensure that the lender will be protected against the mistakes of an unprepared home buyer. Both options

---

will cost you a lot of money that you won't get back. Instead, get into an inexpensive rental situation and get serious about saving for a down payment. Use the other tactics in this book, live as cheap as possible, save up that 20 percent, and then buy. You'll save yourself a tremendous amount of money by exercising some patience.

228. CONSIDER A CHEAPER NEIGHBORHOOD

It's wise to be the richest person in a cheaper neighborhood than to be the poorest person in a rich neighborhood. In the cheaper neighborhood, you won't be surrounded by peer pressure to constantly spend more to keep up with the Joneses. In the expensive neighborhood, you'll constantly be surrounded by temptations to spend money that you don't really have. Look to buy in a less expensive neighborhood at first, and if you're still tempted to move up, save the extra money you're not spending trying to keep up and eventually upgrade. You'll save a ton of money by keeping the expensive Joneses at bay.

229. CONSIDER A CHEAPER PART OF THE COUNTRY

Many areas of the country have prohibitively expensive housing costs that can singly devour any extra income that can be made from living in that area. Look at living in another region of the country, even if it means a reduction in salary. If you can buy a house for $200,000 in Des Moines that would have cost nearly a million in San Francisco, you'll be substantially ahead even if you take a lower paying job. Also, don't merely assume you can't find work in your area of expertise in those other areas. Take a serious look at the job markets in some of the less expensive areas and you might just be very surprised at what you'll find.

230. GET A HUD-1 FORM AND
KNOW WHAT LENDERS WILL BE LOOKING AT

When you start to think about buying a home, request a sample copy of a HUD-1 form at *www.hud.gov*. The HUD-1 form explains in very clear detail exactly what you'll be expected to pay during the process of buying a home, and many people are often surprised by all of the extra fees. Get a copy of this form and learn about each of the items and what you should expect to pay for them. Doing this will help to ensure that you're not hit with some unpleasant surprises when you go to sign the papers, which could cause you to lose an escrow payment or have to take on significant credit card debt to cover things. If you don't understand something, ask questions of any lender that you approach so that you do know what's going on, and also ask for estimates on all of these numbers. Information is key here. Know what you're going into, and you can save a lot of money.

231. GET A SHORTER-TERM MORTGAGE
WITH A LOWER INTEREST RATE

The most important number concerning your mortgage isn't the number of years you'll have to repay it or the amount of your monthly payment, it's the interest rate you'll be paying. The lower the interest rate, the less money you'll be losing to interest payments over the life of your loan and the more money you'll be able to keep in your pocket. When you begin to look at your mortgage options, look seriously at shorter-term options with lower interest rates, like a fifteen-year mortgage. While the monthly payments may be higher, you'll fully own the home in half the time, and by applying many of the other tactics in this book, you'll be able to handle those larger payments.

232. Know Exactly What You Can Afford Before You Look

Before you even start looking at the real-estate listings, sit down and take a long and serious look at your finances. What sort of monthly payment can you realistically afford, especially when including homeowner's insurance, property tax, and upkeep and maintenance costs in the mix? Be realistic in your calculations and know what you really can afford before you even start looking at homes so that you don't waste your time (and tempt yourself) by looking at houses that are more expensive than you can possibly handle. Doing this sort of serious gut check before you even look will save you a lot of money and heartache throughout the buying process.

233. Buy on the Low End of What You Think You Need

When you're out looking at houses, it's very tempting to push what you can afford and get one of the nicer houses. Don't—you'll just be putting the whole thing at risk. Instead, get the less expensive house, which will give you cheaper mortgage payments. Sock the extra money you saved toward home improvements or extra mortgage payments and enjoy the extra breathing room you get from owning a less expensive home. Then, if you're tempted to upgrade later, you'll have improved the value of the house, giving you more leverage to easily handle the leap to a better home.

234. Look for a Fixer-Upper but Avoid Homes with Problems You Can't Fix

One great way to save money when house-shopping is to look for fixer-uppers, homes with minor problems that can be fixed with some effort and time. You can often find great bargains by looking at this category of house, but be realistic about your limitations. Don't buy homes with serious structural integrity problems or problems that involve demolishing pieces of the house to fix properly. If you're looking at options with these kinds of problems and feel like you're up to the task, you're probably better off just building the entire house yourself.

235. Know the Total Cost of the Move Before You Jump

There are many, many hidden costs in moving. Be sure you do an adequate calculation of all of your costs before you make the move, and know what financial resources you'll need so that you're not caught putting thousands of dollars' worth of expenses on a credit card without being able to pay it off easily. Have you considered all of the closing costs listed on your HUD-1 form? Have you considered moving costs? What about the costs for any items you'll need as soon as you move in, such as furniture or other necessary items that you won't be bringing into the house with you? What about the fuel costs of the many trips you'll have to make during the move? How about a small emergency fund to deal with any of the little issues that could happen during the move? These expenses can and will add up, so it's best to be prepared up-front. Make sure all of the costs you can think of are covered by your savings, plus have a small additional emergency fund to handle things you didn't think of. This way, you're not tossing tons of stuff onto a credit card and having to pay high finance charges as you pay them off. Planning ahead saves money, particularly when moving.

236. ASK THE SELLER TO PAY CLOSING COSTS AND OTHER FEES

When you begin to negotiate the closing price of your home, one very useful tactic is to ask the seller to cover your closing costs. This has several benefits. First, it allows the seller to claim a higher sale price for their home, making them feel that they got a better deal (and they can tell their friends that they did). Second, it gives the buyer (you) some breathing room during the expensive closing process. Third, it's often the perfect thing to break an impasse in negotiating, when there's still a gap remaining between what you're willing to pay and what they're willing to offer. Having the seller pay the closing costs can often bridge that gap. In many cases, the end result is that the closing costs are effectively wrapped into the mortgage at a low interest rate, leaving you with cash in hand to take care of the moving costs instead of having to use the cash to cover closing costs and putting your moving costs on credit, which can be incredibly expensive. Paying for closing costs can be a great way for the buyers to keep some cash in their pocket right now while the seller gets the deal done.

237. Shop Around for a Mortgage

When shopping for a mortgage, particularly your first one, it's often tempting to stick with the first friendly person you talk to out of familiarity and nervousness. Don't. Instead, take the time to shop around at several places, including your local credit union. If you can shave an extra 0.5 percent off your mortgage now, it can save you thousands of dollars over the lifetime of your mortgage. There are times in life when doing the legwork really pays off and puts money in your pocket. Shopping around for a mortgage is one of these times. Use *www.bankrate.com* to find out national mortgage rates as well as the rates in your area and use their tools to help you find potential lenders, and don't be afraid to talk to several different lenders to try to find the best deal for you. Be sure, however, that you're not just chasing interest rates. Ask each place for a good faith estimate so that you know how many fees will be tacked on, as a lot of fees can eliminate any interest rate benefit.

238. ATTEND THE HOME INSPECTION YOURSELF AND ASK A LOT OF QUESTIONS

Most home sales today are contingent upon a successful home inspection. While it might be convenient for you to just have the home inspector visit the house while you're at work, don't do it. Go along on the trip, keep your eyes open, and ask lots of questions about everything you're unsure about. Go online and search for a "home inspection checklist," print it, take it with you, and make sure the home inspector goes through each step on the list. Take note of everything the inspector observes and points out to you and follow up on everything, regardless of whether it's your responsibility or the responsibility of the seller. Your home inspection is one of the best opportunities to have someone fully examine your potential home and point out problems. Knowing those problems now can save you tons of money later or possibly even indicate problems severe enough that you back out of the home purchase. Go along, take notes, and pay attention.

239. BE AWARE OF ANY HOMEOWNERS' ASSOCIATIONS OR COVENANTS YOU'LL HAVE TO ADHERE TO

In many neighborhoods, there may be homeowners' associations or covenants that you have to follow and perhaps even pay fees to join. Know what these are before you close the deal or else you may have a nasty financial surprise waiting for you when you move in that may involve home improvements, other requirements, fines, and monthly fees that you didn't expect at all. If you don't know about such arrangements with the home you're buying, ask about them and get a copy of any covenants or agreements that will apply to this home. Any fees or other costs that you're subject to as the owner just add to your housing cost, and they may be enough to tip the scales against buying the property. Find this out up-front so that there's no confusion later on.

240. PRACTICE A MONTHLY HOME MAINTENANCE SCHEDULE

If you already own your home, one way to keep it in good shape (and thus maintain property value and reduce repair expenses) is to start and maintain a monthly home maintenance schedule. Make yourself a checklist of tasks to execute each month in order to keep your home in good shape. Simply do the ones that apply for your home or property.

- ► Check for squeaky doors and oil them as needed
- ► Check and clean range hood filters
- ► Check and replace furnace filters
- ► Check and replace other ventilation system filters
- ► Check and replace humidifier filters

- ► Remove grills on forced air system ducts and vacuum inside the ducts
- ► Examine the foundation for any cracks
- ► Examine exposed wood (for instance, in the attic) for insect damage and do any insect preventive maintenance that needs to happen
- ► Test all ground fault circuit interrupters
- ► Check all vents (inside and outside) and make sure there are no obstructions
- ► Remove screens, clean window wells, and dry them
- ► Examine all outdoor items and see whether any seasonal maintenance needs to be done
- ► Drain off a pan full of water from the clean-out valve at the bottom of your water tank (removes sediment and maintains efficiency)
- ► Check your sump pump for any issues
- ► Test all fire / smoke / carbon monoxide detectors in the house
- ► Check all window and door locks to ensure they're all in working order
- ► Check your fire escape plan and make sure that furniture additions haven't changed this
- ► Check all faucets for dripping water and change washers if needed
- ► Run all sinks, toilets, baths, and showers to ensure no problems (mostly just the ones not used frequently)

- Check the gauge on all fire extinguishers and replace if needed
- Use a pipe cleaner and baking soda to clean all drains
- Check all gutters for blockage and clean as needed (bird's nests, leaves, and so on)
- Check all visible pipes for leaks (don't forget under sinks)
- Check and clean refrigerator and freezer coils (once every six months is sufficient)
- Check all caulking and repair as needed

241. LEARN HOW TO DO SIMPLE HOME MAINTENANCE TASKS

There are countless little tasks around your home that you can do yourself instead of hiring an expensive handyman to take care of them, such as installing a ceiling fan or fixing a faulty light switch. Pick up a general book on home repairs and when a minor issue develops at your home, such as a backed-up drain or a leaky faucet, try repairing the issue yourself using this guide. Most of the time, the fix is incredibly simple and doing it yourself is quick and easy, saving yourself the cost of having a repairman come in and fix it.

242. DON'T OVERSPEND ON A LAWN MOWER OR OTHER HOME MAINTENANCE EQUIPMENT

When you first move into a home, particularly for the first time, you'll be hit with many obvious home and lawn maintenance tasks that need to be handled. Your first tendency will be to go to the local hardware store and pick up equipment to handle the task, but that would not be a cost-effective plan. Instead, hit yard sales and look for this equipment on the cheap. Many people upgrade to riding mowers while push mowers still do the job and will get rid of their older push mower for just a few dollars. If you can get just a year or two of use out of such an old mower, you're ahead, and then you can upgrade your mower on your own terms with proper research to find the best deal. The same policy is true for other maintenance equipment, like weed removers and leaf blowers. Look for them used for your first purchase and upgrade later on when you can do adequate research and get the best bang for the buck.

243. Build Relationships with Your Neighbors

Put in time and effort to build a relationship with the people who live around you, and the relationship will pay off in many ways. A good neighbor will lend you stuff in a pinch, keep an eye on your property when you're traveling, and help you out when you need a hand. If you put effort into cultivating that relationship by being friendly and taking the initiative to do those little things for your neighbor, you will almost always be repaid in kind, and little things like that can subtly save you time, money, and worry over and over again.

244. Consider Building Yourself

A more intense option for people who are looking to upgrade their living space with an eye toward the bottom dollar is to build your home entirely yourself, starting with just a piece of land. In effect, you would serve as your own general contractor, doing the pieces of work that you're most comfortable with and paying others to do the pieces that you're less confident about. This is a huge cost-saver for anyone who is into home repair and doing things themselves. If this is intriguing to you, visit the library and look for books on building your own home. There are many resources available to help get you started on this big project.

245. Consider an Alternative Living Situation

If you're looking to own your own home but simply don't have enough money to do it, consider an alternative living situation. Offer to split costs with close relatives, such as siblings or parents, and have them share the house with you. Consider a group living environment, particularly if you're single and are primarily focused on building your career. If you're living rurally, look into buying a large property with one house on it, then share that home with another family while you build a second home on the other end of the property. Think outside the box a little when it comes to living situations and you can save a great deal of money on your housing costs.

246. Rent Out Unused Rooms

If you live in a home with significantly more space than you need, you can recoup some of your costs by renting out an unused bedroom or other rooms in your home to a student or another person looking for temporary housing. Not only will you be able to earn some income this way, but that person can also help with household chores by reducing the amount of space that needs to be maintained. This can be an excellent option for a person with extra space who could use some help keeping things in order.

247. Downgrade Your Home

Another option to consider if you have more space than you need is downgrading your home. Put your home up for sale and buy a smaller home in a less expensive neighborhood, and not only will you have a house that's more manageable for you with lower bills and upkeep costs, but you'll also have significant proceeds from the sale that you can use to pay off debts or save for the future. Downgrading is a powerful way to live cheap. You can reduce your housing costs while also earning some money from selling the larger house.

hange • Never Be an Early Adopter • Insulate Your Water Heater • Start a Garden • Learn to Love Lefto
Move to a Cheaper Neighborhood • Rent Out Unused Rooms • Check and Replace Furnace Filters • Drive Ca
on Time • Automate Your Savings • Only Wash Full Loads of Dishes or Clothes • Carpool • Air Up All of You

CHEAP TACTIC$ FOR
INSURANCE

248. KNOW YOUR REASONS FOR INSURING

Many people buy insurance on their home, their car, and other things simply because they think they're supposed to do it. With that mindset, you're probably not insuring some things enough and overinsuring other things, resulting in a hodgepodge of policies that aren't adequately protecting you and could be costing you more than they should. Whenever you buy or renew an insurance policy, ask yourself what sort of worst-case scenario this policy is covering, and make sure that scenario is fully covered and nothing more. Investment options and other bells and whistles are unnecessary, just make sure that the things that you need covered are covered. Using this tactic with any insurance you buy will always save you money in the long run while ensuring that you are adequately covered.

249. BUY TERM LIFE INSURANCE

For life insurance, your long-term concern should be that your family is taken care of in the event of your passing. Buy a term life insurance policy with enough value that if you do pass on, your family is financially in good shape. Beyond that, however, avoid other bells and whistles. Don't pay extra to turn your life insurance into a mediocre investment. Instead, use that extra money to keep yourself and your family on a strong financial path.

250. BUY A LONGER-TERM POLICY

When you buy term life insurance, you'll often be given several options with different terms. A shorter-term policy may have lower payments now, but over the long haul, a longer-term policy is a much better deal. Why? In ten years, when the short-term policy runs out, you'll have to get term insurance again, and then you'll be ten years older with the possibility of some health issues that may have arisen between then and now. Buying a policy then, no matter what the length, will be more expensive than buying one now. You're much better off buying a long-term policy now and making slightly higher payments than saving a few bucks now only to pay a lot more later on. The cheap method is to go for the long term.

251. CONSIDER LONG-TERM DISABILITY AND LONG-TERM CARE INSURANCE

Similar to the logic behind life insurance, take a serious look at long-term disability and long-term care insurance, particularly if your family relies on you as a wage earner. This insurance will protect you in the event that you're injured and left unable to perform your previous job. Look into an appropriate long-term disability policy to help replace lost income in the event of such an accident, and match that with a long-term care policy that will pay for any long-term care that you might need if you have medical conditions that require long-term medical care. This insurance covers an unlikely situation, but if something should happen to you, you'll be extremely glad you have this coverage. This is one case where it's often cheaper to spend a little more, just in case.

252. DROP COLLISION AND COMPREHENSIVE COVERAGE ON VERY OLD VEHICLES

If you're driving a very old vehicle, particularly one you're only keeping for emergencies or for future trade-in value, drop comprehensive and collision insurance on that vehicle, keeping only liability coverage. The cost of just a couple years' worth of collision and comprehensive coverage will usually be more than an old car is worth. Making this change will save you money each month that's not being put toward insurance that you almost certainly won't use. With just liability insurance, your car will not be covered if you get into an accident or it needs repairs, but if the car is already near the end of its useful life with many small, impending problems, this isn't a major concern. Save money—go with only liability insurance on very old cars.

253. SHOP AROUND FOR AUTOMOBILE AND HOMEOWNERS' INSURANCE

When you first got your insurance, you may have been getting the best deal around, but is that still true today? It's useful to shop around for rates once every few years just to see if you can save money through another insurance company. Get quotes from several different companies, and use resources like *Consumer Reports* to evaluate their customer service. Remember, though, that if your current insurance company has treated you well so far, it's worth a small premium to stick with them, because a combative insurance company can cause you a great deal of financial hardship.

254. KNOW YOUR DISCOUNTS

When you sign up for insurance, there are often many discounts that you may be eligible for that are stated in the fine print of the policy. Do the research and find all of these discounts and make sure you're getting the ones you're eligible for. Common discounts include a good student discount, a safe driving record (without tickets or accidents), and so on. If you've met the criteria for these, call your insurer and ask for a discount.

255. TRY BUNDLING YOUR POLICIES FOR A DISCOUNT

Many insurance companies offer many different types of insurance—homeowners' insurance, auto insurance, disability insurance, and more all tend to be sold by the same group. Because of this, many insurance companies will offer you a discount if you sign up for multiple types of policies through their organization. Consider doing this, particularly if your current insurer won't offer a bundled package. Any time you need new insurance is a great time to shop around for your existing insurance packages, too, so that you can take advantage of bundled discounts in your calculations.

256. INCREASE YOUR DEDUCTIBLE

Tired of paying high premiums all the time, particularly if you're a safe driver? Look into increasing your deductible—the amount you'll have to pay out of pocket if you do make an insurance claim. Even a slight increase can make a big difference in your premiums. If you don't drive much, consider raising your deductible significantly, as your chances of having severe issues with your car are much lower than if you're a frequent driver.

257. PAY ALL OF YOUR BILLS ON TIME

Insurance bills are incredibly important to keep on top of. Don't be late on a single payment or else a domino effect of negative ramifications may occur: An increase in your premiums, a gap in your coverage, and potential penalties from driving uninsured can all occur, as can a true disaster if you're in an accident or have a breakdown while your insurance has lapsed. Many insurance policies have a grace period for late payments, but don't even push that, as it may still have a negative effect on the premiums that you pay. Don't let your insurance bills get behind or else you'll put yourself at significant risk and also potentially raise your premiums as well.

258. DRIVE CAREFULLY

Defensive driving is important because it keeps you and your passengers safe, but it has the added benefit of keeping your wallet safe as well. Defensive driving can help you avoid accidents, helping you save on repair costs and potential traffic tickets and fines, and also keeps your driving record clean, which helps with insurance costs. Keep your eyes on the road when you're out and about. Avoiding the huge expenses that you can incur by making a mistake pays for the attention you give to driving.

259. KNOW WHAT YOUR REAL REBUILDING COSTS ARE AND PROVIDE PROOF

Have a good idea of the total cost to replace everything that would be destroyed in the event of a disaster. How much is your property worth and how much would it cost to replace it? Make sure you've figured this up with plenty of breathing room before you purchase your policy, and make sure that the amount listed on the policy covers it. *Another tip:* Make a detailed list of all of the contents of your house, with specific descriptions and serial numbers when needed, and keep this in a safe place. You might also want to take a walkthrough video so that other things are captured as well, so you can demonstrate the property that was damaged and needs to be replaced. A bit of preparation now can save you a huge amount of financial heartache later.

260. MAKE YOUR HOME MORE DISASTER RESISTANT

Take some simple steps to decrease the likelihood of devastating disaster in your home, such as adding storm shutters, installing fire alarms, or updating your plumbing and electrical systems. These simple steps will each reduce the likelihood of disaster befalling your home. You can also earn some direct value from actions like these by obtaining a list of disaster resistance tactics from your home insurer along with an estimate on premium reductions you might earn by following these tactics. If you can make a few simple changes to your home to both make it safer and reduce your homeowners' insurance costs, that's a double financial benefit.

261. COMBINE HEALTH INSURANCE WITH YOUR SPOUSE

If you're recently married, look into the possibility of combining your health insurance policy with the one held by your spouse. You might find that your partner has a better policy with smaller copays, plus it may be more cost-effective to have both of you served on the same policy. Similarly, when you add a new member to your family through birth or adoption, look at the various insurance options available to you, including family plans. You may find that a family plan will save your family a substantial amount over individual plans.

262. BYPASS AGENTS AND BUY POLICIES DIRECTLY FROM THE COMPANIES

If you're looking to buy your own insurance policies of any kind (life, health, homeowners', auto, and so on), try contacting the insurance company directly via their website instead of dealing with a local agent. Quite often, you can get a much better deal by bypassing the agent and his referral fees, though the process for signing up may take longer. Use the Internet to your advantage and shop around for different rates directly from the insurance companies themselves, then sign up for that insurance directly.

263. RAISE YOUR CREDIT SCORE

One major factor in determining how much you pay for your insurance premiums is your credit score, which insurance companies will use to estimate how reliable and trustworthy you are. Thus, one quick and effective way to reduce the premiums on your various policies is to raise your credit score. Get a copy of your credit report, review it carefully, and eliminate any problems. Pay all of your bills on time. Keep your credit card debt under control and don't sign up for new cards all the time. Following basic steps for personal finance success will not only help you manage your money better, but it can also result in a nice deduction in your insurance premiums.

264. USE A PAYMENT OPTION THAT LETS YOU PAY THE LEAST AMOUNT TOTAL OVER A YEAR

Most insurance providers give you many ways to pay for this insurance: Monthly payments, quarterly payments, and annual payments are among the common offerings. Don't pay any attention to the option that gives you the smallest individual payments. What's really important is the option that enables you to pay the least amount per year. Multiply the annual payment by twelve, the quarterly payment by four, and the semiannual payment by two in order to make a fair comparison among them, and sign up for the plan that makes you pay the least each year. If you're worried about bills sneaking up on you, start saving automatically for that future bill, taking enough out of your checking each month to make sure you can easily cover that bill when it comes due. The less you pay annually, the less you have to take out of your account each month.

ange • Never Be an Early Adopter • Insulate Your Water Heater • Start a Garden • Learn to Love Left...
Move to a Cheaper Neighborhood • Heat Only Unused Rooms • Check and Replace Furnace Filters • Drive Ca
on Time • Automate Your Savings • Only Wash Full Loads of Dishes or Clothes • Carpool • Air Up All of Your

CHEAP TACTIC$ FOR
LOVE AND MARRIAGE

265. Don't Spend to Impress

Many people tend to want to shell out the cash in order to impress a date right off the bat. That's fine, but if you're spending money solely to impress your date, particularly beyond the first date or two, you're creating an image of yourself that will be difficult to live up to over the long haul. Look for sincere and authentic ways to show your interest that don't involve throwing cash around and creating bogus expectations. Instead of going to the most expensive restaurant in town, ask around and find a great undiscovered place with much more reasonable prices. Instead of just picking something impressive, pay attention to what you know about him or her (and ask friends) to find out what your date genuinely enjoys and focus on doing something related to that. Be real and authentic. Don't let your wallet do the impressing or else you'll make an expensive impression you won't be able to live up to.

266. Give Gifts of Sincerity

When a relationship begins to grow and gift-giving occasions occur, the best option is to always go with a sincere gift from the heart. For example, let's say the person you're dating loves to read. An easy gift idea might be a book that someone at the store suggested that she might like, based on her tastes. A better idea would be a book that is genuinely powerful to you that somehow connects with your relationship. The best gift of all, though, is that book with a note folded up inside explaining just why that book was powerful to you and how it connects to the relationship. Just a little more effort takes an ordinary and unremarkable gift and turns it into something sincere and special that can help build the connection between the two of you. A bit of extra effort and sincerity can make something inexpensive into something truly profound.

267. PLAN A ROMANTIC FREE DATE

If you're committed to living a frugal lifestyle, get your date involved and plan a romantic free date where you don't spend money beyond what you'd ordinarily spend. Pack a backpack full of food, a candle, and some matches and go on an evening hike. Have a movie night where you each pick two films from your own collection and watch all four together. Go on a daylong bicycle ride out in the country together. Spend a Saturday together involved with a volunteer project. Dating doesn't have to be an expensive situation. It just has to be something that you both find value in, and that value doesn't have to cost money.

268. TAKE WALKS TOGETHER

No matter what stage your relationship is in, there are a few things you can do to build a long-term bond, such as taking a long walk together and talking about life, problems, and everything else in between. Relationships are built on a bedrock of communication, and taking a long walk together and giving plenty of open air to revealing things about yourself and getting to know each other on an intimate level can be a big part of that foundation. Communication is the glue that helps people stick together and the best part is that it's free.

269. WRITE LOVE NOTES

To some, this tip might seem very corny, but it's one of the best little things you can do to help keep a relationship alive and vibrant. Every once in a while, when the person you're with least expects it, take a few minutes to write a note simply stating how important that person is to you and then put that note in a place where it will easily be found by the recipient. Little token reminders of your love and affection like this are great, inexpensive ways to refresh the bond between you.

270. BE ATTENTIVE

While it's easy to get caught up in the big things in a relationship, it's often the little things that matter. Pay attention to what your partner is saying and doing, even if it doesn't directly involve you, and use that information to make little choices to make your relationship stronger. For example, instead of plotting a big surprise birthday party for your partner, pay attention and listen to what she really wants. You might find out that the big surprise bash you were thinking about is the last thing on earth that your partner wants and instead she'd rather have a simple and intimate evening alone with you. Another example: If you routinely go out on the town together, an attentive partner might notice that the other person is getting tired of the old routine and thus it might be good for both of you to build a different routine, perhaps one that involves going out less and staying home more. Attentiveness not only builds a relationship, but it often prevents you from throwing away money based on your own preconceptions.

271. FIND AREAS OF MUTUAL INTEREST THAT DON'T INVOLVE SPENDING MONEY

Most relationships are built around some areas of common interest. What areas of common interest do you have with your partner? Which of those areas don't require a great deal of money to enjoy? Put some effort into finding areas of common interest, particularly those that don't require financial input. For example, perhaps you both enjoy bicycle-riding or going on nature walks, or perhaps you're both happy to curl up with a good book. The more time you spend getting to know each other as people, the more likely you are to discover common interests that don't require throwing money to the wind.

272. BUILD A FINANCIALLY EQUAL RELATIONSHIP FROM THE START

Obviously, no relationship will start off with both partners on exactly equal financial footing, but that doesn't mean that a healthy relationship revolves around one person covering all of the necessary bills while the other member is a spendthrift. Instead, both partners should take responsibility for some part of the financial situation and both partners should also get to reap some of the reward in terms of financial flexibility and spending money. You can start this early on by having both partners occasionally paying for date expenses, or by going Dutch regularly. Later on, agree to have one person cover a few of the bills while the other person covers the rest. For example, one partner might pay for rent while the other one handles the other expenses. Eventually, you'll want to merge finances with some basic agreements and rules on how things work for both partners. Doing this now will save much pain and needless expense later on, as both partners are committed to and involved with the financial success of each other.

273. GET ON THE SAME PAGE FINANCIALLY

Beyond merely working together to get the bills paid, it also helps to talk about long-term goals and what you both can do to reach these goals together. What do you both dream about? Where do you see yourselves in ten years? Set some big goals that you both have an interest in achieving, and then offer each other positive encouragement toward reaching those goals. Encourage each other to reduce spending and make intelligent purchasing decisions. Talk about the temptations that you each have, and confess your fears and challenges to your partner as well. Put everything out there on the table—everything you're worried about, everything that makes you uncomfortable, everything you dream about. Work together to break down those worries and move toward those dreams. Knowing that you're both on the same page with similar goals and pushing each other in a loving way toward those goals will save both of you a tremendous amount of money over the long run and will also help cement a lifelong relationship.

274. Plan a Wedding Centered Around Loved Ones, Not Stuff

Many wedding plans grow completely out of control, costing the bride and groom and their family many thousands of dollars for one over-the-top day. In the end, though, memories aren't made of a ten-foot cake or of the perfect flower arrangement or of the expensive bridesmaids' dresses. The memories are about friends and family coming together to celebrate. Your wedding plans should focus on the people you love and care about, not on some giant fairytale wedding fueled by bridal industry marketing. Instead of asking how big your wedding cake should be, ask whether or not the wedding and reception will be accessible to everyone. Instead of picking out the "perfect" dress for the bridesmaids to wear, pick them out together and make a price-conscious choice that reflects the financial realities of everyone involved. Another option is to drastically shrink the entire wedding plan and have an incredibly simple ceremony, surrounded only by the people you care about the most.

275. Plan a Romantic Honeymoon,
Not an Expensive One

Many marriages start off with a pricey honeymoon that goes far beyond what the new couple can rationally afford. While a honeymoon can be a truly memorable experience, it doesn't have to come at the expense of financial reality. Instead of planning an expensive "destination" honeymoon, plan something simple that you'll both deeply enjoy. Love wine? Tone a trip to Paris down to a week-long driving tour of the Napa and Sedona Valleys. Enjoy the outdoors? Spend your honeymoon together in a stunning national park, enjoying natural beauty during the day and each other at night. Just want to get away? Spend it away from everyone in a small, quiet town in your favorite area of the country where you can enjoy yourself deeply on a shoestring. Your honeymoon doesn't have to have five stars or a five-figure bill. Step back from that concept and look at what you're both really passionate about, and ask yourself how you can share that passion together in an intimate setting. You'll find your answer there, and it'll likely save you a lot of money over the usual honeymoon ideas.

276. Don't Get Married if
You're Still Having Doubts

If you're nearing your wedding day and you're still feeling intense doubts about the whole idea, don't get married. For starters, if you're unsure about the whole idea, there's a strong chance that once you're married, your marriage will fail and you'll have to face the deep financial and emotional cost of divorce. For another reason, if your partner is committing with his or her whole heart and you're not doing the same, you're being truly unfair to that person, taking their hopes and dreams and passions and not giving the same in return. If you feel doubts, take the time and space you need to work through them, but don't commit to marriage unless you're truly ready to give it your all. Marriage isn't easy and ending a marriage can be incredibly expensive. Don't make that commitment unless it's with your whole heart.

277. GIVE YOUR MARRIAGE THE CARE AND FEEDING IT NEEDS

Once you're settled into married life, don't abandon the things that made your relationship work to begin with. Spend time every day, or as often as you possibly can, with your partner just talking about your cares and concerns. Engage in activities together as often as you can, and if you notice you're starting to do more things apart, make a concerted effort to steer that ship back in the right direction by suggesting things to do together. Forgive your partner for little mistakes. Your partner's not perfect and neither are you. Putting forth the regular effort to keep your relationship strong will not only make your marriage last, but it will save you the money and heartache of counseling and potentially the money and heartache of a painful divorce.

278. Realize Money Doesn't
Heal a Marital Problem

Many people try to repair rifts in relationships by throwing money at the problem. A big bouquet of flowers, a wonderful gift, and a kiss on the cheek and suddenly everything is better, right? While a gift might appear to be a good patch, it's just superficial—the real problem often goes much, much deeper. If you find yourself in a situation where you're plotting to "fix" things by buying a gift, ask yourself honestly whether you're actually trying to fix the problem or if you're just hoping to smooth things over without really fixing anything at all. If you're just trying to smooth things over, a different approach might be in order. Instead of buying an expensive gift, set aside some time to talk with your spouse about the problem and listen to what your spouse says. Take it seriously. If passions are on display, then it's because something is important. Don't just buy something. Not only is it a waste of money in the end, it does nothing at all to actually heal the problem.

279. Be Completely Honest with Your
Partner about Money Issues

When you're dealing with finances, complete honesty is always the best policy. It's far better to show your partner that bill you're hiding now than to hold on to it until later when months of dishonesty have built up around it (and a higher balance has likely built up as well). If you're ashamed to tell your partner about a purchase you've made, you're better off talking about it now than convincing yourself that it's really fine and opening the door to a Pandora's box of spending. Whenever you spend money, you should be willing to tell your spouse about it, and if you are truly open, it will encourage your spouse to be equally open.

280. HAVE REGULAR TALKS ABOUT YOUR FINANCIAL SITUATION

Once every month or so, sit down with your partner and talk about your financial situation. Go through your bills together, allowing your partner to see exactly what you spend and you to see exactly what your partner spends. Talk about your progress toward your big goals and encourage each other to keep making good moves all the time. Doing this regularly encourages you both to make better financial moves on a daily basis, reducing unnecessary spending and thinking more about the big goals that you share, which in the long run is an incredibly financially strong way to live.

281. ENCOURAGE YOUR PARTNER'S FRUGALITY

Make a regular effort to encourage your partner to spend less money on frivolous things and make smarter buying decisions. If your partner made a tight grocery list, went to the store, and cut your usual grocery store bill in half, compliment him on the good move. If your partner is trying to choose between different items, encourage her to choose the less expensive one. If you're evaluating a new appliance together, look for energy-efficient and reliable models on sale and point these things out to your partner. Suggest activities together that don't require money and be optimistic and positive when your partner does the same. Rely on each other for living cheap and you'll both do much better.

282. SHOW YOUR LOVE FREQUENTLY INSTEAD OF SOMETHING BIG ONCE IN A WHILE

Culture has taught us that big gifts on certain occasions are the way to go, but those gifts are often put up on a pedestal, far out of proportion as a symbol of love. Instead of focusing on a diamond ring or an absurdly expensive set of golf clubs, once every few years, look for smaller things that you can do more often to show your partner that you care. Don't worry about the expensive diamond necklace. Just put a note on her pillow every once in a while, give her a kiss and an "I love you" when you see her for the first time in the evening, or stick a bar of her favorite chocolate in her purse to surprise her sometimes. Don't focus on the amazing new gadget. Instead, make him his favorite sandwich and bring it to him when he doesn't expect it, encourage him to spend an afternoon just twiddling around by himself out in the garage when he's feeling restless, or surprise him with your passion at an unexpected moment. Those little things don't cost much at all, take the pressure away from an over-the-top "big" gift that could push some financial buttons, and helps keep your marriage alive and happy, all in one swoop.

283. MAKE SURE THAT YOU'RE BOTH ON THE SAME PAGE WHEN IT COMES TO CHILDREN

A final tip about relationships: Address the question of whether to have children openly and deeply, and only commit to having children if you're both ready and committed to it. Children can be incredibly expensive and also incredibly demanding of your time, but the emotional and personal rewards of parenthood are many. Even knowing this, it's not a tradeoff that some people want to make, and others may hide their reluctance in an effort to please their spouse. A child born into a situation where both parents aren't committed to the child can create an uncomfortable situation for everyone, one that might lead to separation and divorce. Not only would this be financially and emotionally devastating to you, but it's also wholly unfair to the child, who wasn't involved with the choice at all. Carefully consider the child question, be open about it, and listen to what your partner has to say. It's perhaps the biggest decision you'll have to make—only make the leap when you're both on the same page.

CHEAP TACTIC$ FOR
SOCIALIZING

284. Join a Community Organization

Your best opportunity to meet up with a group of people who share your common interests is to join a community organization, such as Toastmasters, the Lion's Club, and so forth. Stop by city hall and ask if you can find a list of active organizations in your community and request contact information for those groups to find out more. Try visiting the websites and attending the meetings (if allowed) of a few groups to find out about them, then look into becoming involved with any organizations that do click with you. Most organizations provide a great positive way to get involved with your community, meet new and interesting people, improve yourself, and do it all for a very low cost.

285. Attend Community Events and Actively Participate

There are also many events held in communities every week that are open to the public where you can not only get involved in what's going on in your community, but you can also meet many people who are interested in the community as well. Check the community calendar and find out what sorts of community events are going on in your area this week, then dip your toes into any that might be of interest to you, from local politics (city council and school board) to cultural festivals. Introduce yourself to people and don't be afraid to ask questions. If an event doesn't "click" with you, try something else until you find a community event that does.

286. GET INVOLVED IN YOUTH ACTIVITIES

Another approach for meeting new people in your community, particularly if you're a parent, is getting involved in the organization of youth activities. Volunteer to coach a youth sport. Participate in the PTA. Volunteer to help out with youth camps or to be a group leader in a youth organization. You'll not only get the opportunity to be involved in a productive effort that helps out young people, but you'll also get the social opportunity to get to know many parents whose children are involved in such activities. If you have children of your own, it can also provide an opportunity to get to know many of the parents of your child's peers, people you will naturally have common interests with.

287. JOIN A VOLUNTEER ORGANIZATION

Another angle to take on the whole socialization-through-involvement tactic is to join a volunteer organization that works in your community or in neighboring ones. Get involved with your local soup kitchen or food pantry. Volunteer to participate regularly in any Habitat for Humanity projects in your area. Volunteer your time at the local animal shelter. Get involved in efforts to maintain gardens in local parks. Get involved in encouraging people to vote, or join a political campaign as a volunteer. There are volunteer efforts for almost any interest you might have, and every volunteer effort is a collection of people passionate about the same thing, meaning you immediately have something in common. It's a way to meet new people, spend some time doing something personally compelling, and best of all, it's free.

288. JOIN A BOOK CLUB

Enjoy reading, but also value interacting with other people? Look around for community book clubs and join one. Start your search at the library. Most libraries have at least one book club, and many have several book clubs spread out over many different areas of interest. Many library book clubs have enough books (through interlibrary loans and so on) so that all members can check out the books, so there's usually no cost involved—plus you can meet interesting people who are genuinely enthusiastic about reading and sharing their thoughts on books. Book clubs are an incredible social opportunity for avid readers.

289. TAKE LEADERSHIP POSITIONS

If you find an organization that really clicks with you, volunteer within those groups to take on leadership positions. This opportunity will not only give you more activities to spend your time on, but it will also provide many opportunities for additional social interactions, give you an opportunity to build strong relationships with other people who care deeply about the organization or the cause, and possibly provide a résumé builder, all for free. If you're involved, don't hesitate to get on a committee, head up a task force, or run for an office within the group.

290. Host a Potluck Dinner

Potluck dinners are a great way to get a group of friends together and enjoy a meal and a social evening with minimal cost for all involved. Just call up your friends, invite them over to dinner, and have them bring a side dish or some other element of the meal. Not only does this provide an inexpensive dinner for all involved, but it also sets the stage for a fun social evening. Better yet, get a regular potluck dinner going on a rotating basis among a group of friends.

291. Host a Game Evening

Don't want to mess with a meal? Host an evening where people come over to your house to play cards or a well-known game, such as Pictionary. Ask people to bring beverages and you have an evening's worth of fun with a group of friends for free. Keep the idea fresh by having different people host the event with different games, and make an effort to keep the games simple and open to everyone but still intriguing enough to reward repeat play. Some ideas and examples: trick-taking card games, Pictionary, and Monopoly.

292. Host a Sporting Event Party

Another great way to get a social crowd together without a great deal of expense is to host a sporting event party. Invite a long list of people to come and bring a beverage and/or a finger food and the expenses become minimal, plus the environment at such events is almost always upbeat, festive, and fun. Sure, you probably have some cleanup effort afterward, but if you host one party, you'll likely be invited to many others, which gives you a long chain of inexpensive or free social events to enjoy.

293. HOST A BLOCK PARTY

One effective way to get to know your neighbors better is to host a block party, where you invite over all of the people who live near you. Usually, this can take the form of a potluck, where everyone who attends brings a side dish, while the host provides a central dish or beverages. While this can be a bit of an expense, it also provides a stellar opportunity to get to know the people who live around you and can also provide the initiative for a series of such parties. Hosting a block party can initiate friendships, plus encourage others to do the same, both of which open the door to many other social opportunities.

294. BUILD FRIENDSHIPS WITH PARENTS OF YOUR CHILDREN'S FRIENDS

If you're a parent, you'll be interacting with your child's friends and, inevitably, their parents. It's a good idea to make a social effort to get to know the parents of your children's friends. One way to do this is to simply invite their family over for dinner, which they can reciprocate later on. This allows the children to play together and the parents to get to know each other a bit. If a friendship takes hold, it can be a tremendously useful thing for both families, giving them each a known safe place for their children to go, plus a potential strong friendship. In the worst case, you find out more about your child's friends with only the cost of a few home-cooked meals, but in the best case, you begin to build a lasting friendship. That's an incredibly valuable investment.

295. WHEN MAKING A MAJOR PURCHASE, TAP YOUR SOCIAL NETWORK

If you've put effort into hosting some social events, you'll likely have built a social network without spending money like crazy. Once you have that social network, it can pay off time and time again. For example, if you're about to make a major purchase, like a new appliance or a new automobile, call around and ask your friends for advice. What appliances work for them? Do they have any sellers that they recommend? Not only will you get honest and useful advice, you might also find that a friend of yours had a friend who can get you a great deal on what you're looking for, saving you a ton of money. Even if that doesn't happen, you'll have built upon the trust of your friendship simply because you asked for their help, plus you'll have some good advice to work with when moving forward with your big purchase.

296. OFFER TO TRADE SKILLS WITH YOUR FRIENDS

Another effective way to save money with your friends is to offer to trade skills with them. What skills do you have to offer? Perhaps you're good with computers, while you have a friend who's good at electrical wiring—you're a systems support specialist and your friend is an electrician. Offer to tune up your friend's computer in exchange for his assistance in installing a ceiling fan—both of you save money. Making this successful is easy: Know what your friends do professionally and what their primary hobbies are, and let them know that you're willing to help them out by providing whatever skills you have. The likelihood is that over the long run you'll both save money by sharing your skills.

297. ORGANIZE "WORK PARTIES" WHERE PEOPLE GATHER TO HELP WITH A TASK

Do you have a major task that needs to get done, like laying new cement for a basketball court or re-shingling your roof? Utilize the social network you've built and invite a group of your friends over to help out. Provide refreshments and be willing to offer your help to them if they need it for similar large projects. You can transform a large, arduous task into a fun social event for a large group of people. The key is to be willing to do the same for the people you invite; in fact, if you hear about a friend who is organizing such a "work party," volunteer to help out. You're much more likely to get people involved in your task if you show a repeated willingness to help others out. In either case, a "work party" can be a very inexpensive and fun way to spend an afternoon, plus it can save you a lot of money if it helps you get a major task done with minimal expense.

298. Share Purchases of Equipment with Neighbors and Friends

Do you have a large yard and need a riding lawn mower? Are any of your friends in a similar situation? Look into sharing the cost of a major purchase, then sharing the use of the item equally. Doing this gives you full use of the equipment that you need with only half the cost and half of the repair expense when it breaks down, or even less if you get a third or a fourth friend involved in the purchase. *A tip:* If you do enter into this type of an arrangement, clearly specify between you what the ground rules are for use, who will store it, how the other person can easily access it, and so on. Be a bit flexible and you can wind up saving yourself thousands of dollars.

299. Share Money-Saving Tips with Your Friends

If you discover a clever way to save some money, share it with your friends. Tell them about the great idea you've implemented and how much money it's saved you. Then, when they discover a clever way to save money, they're likely to share this idea with you, which you can then implement to save money as well. Sharing such ideas can be a great way to touch base with friends while at the same time discovering new ideas for reducing your bottom line.

300. Buy in Bulk with Friends

Bulk buying can save you a lot of money, but it's hard to get through all of the material that you purchase before it begins to go bad.

You can solve that problem by arranging bulk purchases with your friends, splitting the cost of the item and the purchase itself. For example, if you can save 20 percent by buying an enormous box of cereal, split the cost with a friend, then divide the box in half (with half remaining in the box and the other half in a container) when you get home. That way, you each have the contents of a normal-sized box of cereal with a 20 percent discount. You can do the same thing with almost any bulk purchase that you both agree on. Visit a warehouse store together and select items as a team.

301. HOST AN ALL-DAY "COOK AHEAD" PARTY

Eager to try cooking meals in advance but the time investment seems tremendous? Want to take even more advantage of bulk buying of ingredients? Host a "cook ahead" party at your house, where each person brings a huge amount of a few ingredients, then you all work together to assemble a bunch of meals that can be frozen for future easy cooking. Casseroles work really well for this, as do soups and stews. Figure out some recipes, call up some friends, assign some items for each person to get, and have a giant cooking party. It can be social fun while saving you all money on food and time later on, when evenings are busy.

hange • Never Be an Early Adopter • Insulate Your Water Heater • Start a Garden • Learn to Love Leftovers
Move to a Cheaper Neighborhood • Rent Out Unused Rooms • Check and Replace Furnace Filters • Drive Car
an Time • Automate Your Savings • Only Wash Full Loads of Dishes or Clothes • Carpool • Air Up All of Your

CHEAP TACTIC$ FOR
SHOPPING

302. Don't Shop for Entertainment's Sake

One of the biggest social temptations that people face is the idea of shopping for entertainment's sake. Heading out to the mall with friends, credit card in hand, or hitting the golf or electronics shop with your buddy are sure ways to convince yourself to spend extra money. If you don't have a distinct purchase you need to make, don't go to a shopping center. Instead, find another activity to do, one that doesn't constantly encourage you to bust out the plastic for things you don't really need.

303. Discover Craigslist and Freecycle

If you're unfamiliar with these services, get familiar. They're both tremendous ways for you to save money on items. Craigslist (*www .craigslist.com*) is essentially a giant free online classified ad service that often lists items at tremendous discounts or for free if you'll just come and get them. Freecycle (*www.freecycle.com*) is a series of local listings where people list things that they're wanting to get rid of, while others list requests for items that they'd like to receive. Visit these sites, browse the listings, and get a feel for the stuff that's available. You'll likely find some tremendous bargains, as well as a way to get rid of your unwanted stuff and find a happy home for it.

304. Get into Free Customer Programs

If a store you frequent regularly has a free customer rewards or a frequent buyer program, sign up for it. First, before you go to the store, sign up for a free Gmail account (*http://gmail.google.com*) to give yourself a free address with which to collect the e-mails they may send out. Then, sign up for any free programs at any stores you visit. Always list this new e-mail address in the email field. Then, on a regular basis, check that e-mail address and see what offers have been sent to you. Always check it if you're about to head to that store with a specific purchase in mind—you may have an appropriate discount just waiting for you.

305. TRY WAREHOUSE SHOPPING

Another effective way to save money is to try warehouse shopping at one of the many warehouse "members only" clubs, like Costco or Sam's Club. Call your local store and see if you can get a guest pass (some clubs offer these; others do not), then take your old grocery receipt in there with you to compare prices. Compare the prices you regularly pay with the regular prices in the warehouse club—some may be the same, but many may be lower. Depending on your purchasing habits, you can easily save $10 to $20 per shopping trip at a warehouse club, and if that's the case, a membership in such a club will quickly pay for itself.

306. USE THE "ONE MONTH" COUPON STRATEGY

The coupon section in your Sunday newspaper can be a treasure trove of savings, but only if you use it effectively. Many items that you see coupons for are in the midst of a promotional campaign that will often include in-store sales as well at a later date, usually a month or so later. So, to maximize the value of these coupons, clip the good ones now and hold onto them for a while. Compare your coupon hoard with the store flyer each week to see if any of them match up, then add that item to your grocery list and take the coupon with you. Doing this as a regular habit can get you many items for mere pennies, particularly if you check the flyers from drugstores (like Walgreen's and CVS) and discount grocery stores for good coupon matches.

307. Use the Internet for More Coupons

Many websites offer coupons as well. Some of the more popular coupon sites, such as Coupons.com (*www.coupons.com*), offer a bevy of coupons for all sorts of products. Go through those sites, looking for coupons for products you already use or coupons that seem to create a tremendous discount on the product, and print them out to add to your coupon hoard. You can also directly visit the website of your favorite stores, as many of them offer in-store coupons to save even more money on specific products.

308. Double Savings with Manufacturer and Store Coupons

If you find a manufacturer coupon and a store coupon for the same item, you're in luck. Almost all stores will honor both coupons, meaning you can often double your savings with little effort. Thus, checking on both manufacturer and store coupons can be incredibly valuable, sometimes netting you free and almost-free items. If you're doing coupon searches online, open up two browser windows, one with a manufacturer coupon site like Coupons.com, and another with the website of your favorite retailer. Compare the coupons on both, and print out any coupons that appear in both forms, as quite often these add up to a free or nearly free item.

309. WAIT ON PURCHASES UNTIL SALES APPEAR

If you're considering a larger purchase, particularly of an item that's not a hot new release, practice a bit of patience before you make your purchase. Shop around and wait for a sale to crop up. For example, if you're considering buying a DVD player, don't just run down to the store and pick one up. Be patient and wait for the DVD players to go on sale. Waiting a month or two won't be the end of the world, particularly if it saves you some cash.

310. USE STORE FLYERS TO IDENTIFY THOSE SALES

The easiest way to find these sales is to hit the store flyers each week. Pick up a Sunday paper (which usually has dozens of store flyers inside) and examine each one for the item you're considering buying. If you don't find the item you're thinking of purchasing, wait until next week. This saves you the effort of searching in multiple stores for a particular item over and over again. Instead, let the sale come to you via the flyers.

311. Use a Price Book for Your Regular Purchases

Most people fall into a routine of buying thirty or so items on a very regular basis, sometimes during every shopping trip. Items like milk, eggs, laundry detergent, toothpaste, and bread are common purchases for most people, and many people often have a preferred choice or two within these items. One way to subtly save yourself money on these regular items is to start a price book, a brilliant tactic made famous by Amy Dacyczyn in her *Tightwad Gazette* newsletter in the 1990s. All you do is make a list of all of those items you buy regularly, then write down the price for that item at each of several different grocery stores in the area. You'll usually get a clear picture of where the discounts are, and it can help you select the cheapest store to shop at by default as well as a tool to compare your shopping list with, because there may be a cheaper store to shop at depending on the exact items you're buying that week.

312. Shop Alone

Unless you're shopping specifically to split purchases with a friend, try to shop alone. The more people you have along on a shopping trip, the easier it is for impulse buys to slip into the cart, as there's many more opportunities for impulsiveness with multiple people than there is with one person. A single person equipped with a planned shopping list has the least chance to slip an impulsive purchase into the cart, so go alone to save some money in the checkout aisle.

313. Set a "Time Goal"
When You Walk in the Door

If you're entering a store where you know you're likely to be distracted (like a clothing store, an electronics store, or a bookstore), set a time goal when you need to check out and leave the store. This will reduce the opportunities you have to be distracted by impulsive buys and keep you focused on the items you're intending to purchase. One effective way to do this is to set the alarm clock on your watch or on your phone, so that it beeps loudly, reminding you that it's time to get out of the store and making sure you're not dawdling.

314. Only Buy the Specific Item(s)
You're Shopping For

If you go into an electronics store specifically to buy a particular cable for your home entertainment system, don't walk out of the store with anything but that cable. If you go into a bookstore looking for a particular Stephen King novel, don't walk out the door with anything in your hands other than a Stephen King novel. When you enter a store with one or two purchases in mind and walk out with anything more than that, you're falling for the trap of impulse buying, which subtly eats your money and leaves you with nothing but stuff you really didn't need and a big fat bill. If you spy something that you want while in a store, take note of it, but don't buy it. Instead, use tip #7 and see if you even remember the item at all in thirty days. You more likely won't remember anything other than the money you saved that stayed in your pocket.

315. DON'T BUY ANY ITEM IN THE CHECKOUT AISLE

Stores love to load their checkout aisle with impulse buys. Candy that's attractive to both children and adults, magazines aimed at tickling your fancy by shocking and surprising you enough to pick them up and add them to your cart, small overpriced versions of very common purchases such as batteries that you might see and exclaim, "Oh, I forgot, I needed those," and so on. The easiest rule of thumb for protecting your wallet is to not buy anything at all in the checkout. Make it a hard-and-fast rule. Once you head for the checkout, nothing else goes in your cart unless it's on your list. If you see something in the checkout that you remember that you needed (like those aforementioned batteries), don't just grab those. Either head back to the battery area and look at a more well-rounded selection of options or simply add batteries to your list for your next shopping trip.

316. SHOP ON YOUR STATE'S TAX-FREE HOLIDAYS

Many states offer tax-free holidays, where you can buy certain items such as clothing or books without paying sales tax on those items. Not only that, many stores have sales on those days, because they know that people will tend to go out and shop on those days more than on other days. If you have any purchases that you know you need to make, such as clothing purchases, find out if your state has an upcoming tax holiday and hold off on your purchase until then. When the day approaches, find out about sales on the items you're looking at and find the best opportunity to get the items you're looking for with both the benefit of a sale and without the cost of sales tax.

317. Shop Online for Better Price Comparisons

Whenever you're looking to buy any nonperishable item, particularly one that costs more than a few dollars, always do price comparisons online before buying. Utilize the websites of your preferred stores as well as the websites of online retailers and seek out the best price for the item you want. The more expensive the item, the more valuable this comparison shopping can be. You can often save 10 to 15 percent off the purchase price of an item (or even more) with just a few moments of comparison shopping. For just a few minutes' worth of footwork, that can be a very solid return.

318. Don't Store Your Credit Card with an Online Shopping Site

If you get into the routine of buying items online, it's very easy to store your credit card number there, making it incredibly simple to buy things with a click and ship them to your home, no fuss, no muss. The convenience, though, is a clever trap. The quicker you can go from selecting an item to having bought it, the less time you have to actually think about what you're buying and the more likely you are to just go ahead with a completely impulsive and unnecessary purchase. The easiest thing you can do is simply not store your credit card number on a retail website, so that you have to re-enter your number each time you make a purchase. Doing this effectively works like the ten-second rule (tip #6). It makes you pause for a bit and think about what you're actually buying, and that's often enough to make you realize that you're making an impulsive decision. You'll put your credit card away and happily realize that you just made the frugal choice.

319. DON'T BUY "JUST ONE MORE THING" TO GET FREE SHIPPING

Online shopping sites commonly offer free shipping if you spend beyond a certain dollar value, and when you're close to that amount it's often tempting to just find one more item to buy to push yourself over that threshold. Don't. Buying an item just to fill up a slot in your cart means that you're spending more money overall just to get an item you don't really want. Instead, just pick the low-end shipping (since that's what free shipping is) and be glad that you didn't waste $8 on some item you didn't really want just to get "free" shipping. In the end, free shipping isn't really free at all if it makes you spend more money to buy more stuff you don't need.

320. If Prices are Equal, Buy at Your Local Store

If you do a price comparison between online stores and local retail shops and find the prices to be the same, buy at your local retail shop. Why? There's extra value at your local retailer. Salespeople who can answer questions and help with setup, and the store is a place to easily return a faulty product, for starters. In terms of customer service, you get much more value from your local brick-and-mortar retailer than you do from an online service because you can actually communicate face to face with the retailer, tap their knowledge, and take advantage of their return policy and other services they might offer. Buying local puts more value with your product than buying online, so when all else is equal, buy local.

g Exchange * Never Be an Early Adopter * Insulate Your Water Heater * Start a Garden * Learn to Love Left
ter * Move to a Cheaper Neighborhood * Rent Out Unused Rooms * Check and Replace Furnace Filters * Dr
Bills on Time * Automate Your Savings * Only Wash Full Loads of Dishes or Clothes * Carpool * Air Up All o

CHEAP TACTIC$ FOR
UTILITIES AND BILLS

321. ELIMINATE ANY MONTHLY SERVICES
YOU DON'T USE

Take a look at all of your monthly bills. Are any of those bills going to cover services that you don't use or that you use only once in a while? Ask yourself some hard questions about your services. Do you rarely watch television? If so, why are you paying a cable bill? If you don't use your landline telephone at all, scratch that service. Similarly, if you don't use a cell phone, scratch that. Perhaps you can replace a bill with a cheaper alternative; for example, if you've got both an Internet bill and a landline bill, ditch the land line and use a VOIP (voice-over-Internet protocol) phone service like Skype or Vonage at a cheaper rate.

322. TAKE A HARD LOOK AT
CLUB MEMBERSHIP FEES AND GYM FEES

Are you a member of the local country club or gym? Do you use that service, or is it something that you keep open because you might use it someday? If it's just a "someday" service, take the initiative and cancel the membership, because it's just eating at your money without providing you any benefit in return. If you do change your mind and decide to utilize the service, you can always sign up for the service again, but most likely you'll walk away happy knowing that you're spending significantly less each month on something you didn't really use.

323. Take a Hard Look at Entertainment-Oriented Monthly Bills

Are you subscribed to a DVD rental club? Do you pay for premium movie channels? Are you involved in a book-of-the-month club in the mail? Regular bills for entertainment purposes are great places to look for areas where you can reduce spending. Ask yourself how much you honestly use these services and whether or not the monthly bill you pay is really worth it. Explore alternatives for the same thing. Perhaps you can rent a few videos locally each month for less money, or maybe a trip to the library once a month might sate your reading desire as well as or better than a book-of-the-month club. If you're paying a bill every month just to entertain yourself, ask yourself if there's not a better option available that isn't a constant drain on your budget.

324. Clean Up Your Remaining Bills

After you've eliminated some of your regular bills, look for options to clean up your remaining bills. Go through those bills and look for optional services that you rarely or never use. Don't text message? Eliminate buying text messages for your phone. Don't use Internet access? Eliminate that service. Don't watch channels outside of basic cable? Downgrade your cable or satellite package. Paying an arm and a leg for child care? Look for another provider, or see whether or not you can change your schedule to reduce the number of days you're paying for. Pay for a session at the salon every few weeks? Cut it back to once every other month and get a less maintenance-heavy cut. Simple moves like these cut down your bills, giving you more breathing room each month. Just downgrading some services can move you from treading water to making progress against your debts.

325. IF YOU GO OVER YOUR CELL PHONE MINUTES, UPGRADE YOUR PLAN

If you're ever over on your cell phone minutes during a "normal" month (not one with a particularly exceptional event that won't be repeated), call your cell phone provider and upgrade your plan to include more minutes. An overage during a normal month is often a sign that future overages will occur in the coming months as you're beginning to use your cell phone more than you used to. Don't get eaten alive by overage fees. Get a plan that covers your actual cell phone usage and don't sweat it.

326. IF YOU RACK UP "OUT OF CALLING AREA" CHARGES, UPGRADE YOUR PLAN

If you begin to rack up regular "out of calling area" charges on your cell phone bill (more than once or twice a year), then it's time to upgrade your cell plan from a small region to a larger one—or perhaps to a nationwide plan. It only takes a few calls outside your calling area each year to eat up the entire difference in the cost of the plans, so if you find yourself beginning to make out-of-area calls on a regular basis, look at another plan. It will save you money over the long haul.

327. Avoid Long-Term Contracts

Many services you sign up for, particularly cell phones, gyms, cable, and satellite radio and television, require that you sign a contract to use the service for some specified length of time. While it might seem like a better deal to sign a long-term contract because of a slightly lower rate, don't. Keep your contract short. This gives you the freedom to cut your relationship with them much earlier if you're not happy with the service or you're not using it regularly enough to justify the expense. Plus, with shorter contracts, you have more freedom to jump to other providers and enjoy very lucrative introductory offers. Long-term contracts are only a good deal if you're very happy with the service that a particular company offers and you know you'll be happy with that company more than with other companies for a long time to come.

328. Ask for Introductory Deals, Even if You're a Regular Customer

Whenever you're shopping around for services from vendors, look at the introductory deals available to new customers, particularly those that also apply to shorter-term contracts. Introductory deals can often save you a bundle. Don't stop there, though. If you discover a new introductory deal offered by a company you're already with, call them and ask for that same introductory deal for yourself. This works best near the end of your contract with them, as the introductory deal can be applied to a renewal of your previous contract. Don't be afraid to ask. The worst they can do is say no, and if they say yes, you save a bundle. Don't know how to find introductory deals? Do some online searching on occasion to see what's out there by searching for the name of the provider and the phrase "introductory offer."

329. LEVERAGE COMPETING DEALS

Similarly, if you're about to sign a new contract or renew an existing one, shop around beforehand for offers from various companies and try to use them for leverage. Bring in an introductory offer or advertised rate from another company and ask your current company to match or beat it. Either they do agree to match the price, which means you save money and get to continue with the service and equipment you already have, or they refuse, which opens the door to you to switch to that better offer. You may have to be upfront about this in order to achieve success. One strong tactic is to ask to talk to a supervisor if you hear an initial refusal to match the offer. Many companies will try very hard to keep you as a customer, so use an opportunity to switch companies as an opportunity to save some money.

330. Ask about Termination Fees

Whenever you're about to sign a contract, make sure you're very clear on the termination fees associated with that contract. Why? There may come a situation, particularly early in the contract, where it's more cost-effective to terminate the contract, pay the termination fee, and move to another contract with another group. Also, know about the situations in which the termination fee doesn't apply, for example, if you move to an area without adequate service for your phone or if they change your contract (which should give you a window of opportunity to terminate the contract). Knowing when you can terminate without a fee can save you a bundle, particularly when it enables you to quickly sign up for an introductory deal elsewhere.

331. If You Receive Large, Irregular Bills, Save for Them Automatically

Many of the regular bills people face don't come on a monthly basis. Tax bills often come annually or semiannually, as do insurance bills. For most people on a tight budget, bills like these are devastating. They force you to buy regular things on credit and then get saddled with finance charges on the credit card as you pay it down. The most effective method to handle bills that come irregularly is to automatically put away a fraction of the cost of that bill every month. Contact your bank and ask if you can set up automatic deposits into a savings account each month. For an annual bill, put away $\frac{1}{12}$ of the bill amount into a savings account each month (just divide the bill total by 12). For a semiannual bill, put away ⅙ of the bill amount into a savings account each month. If you have your bank do this automatically, you'll barely notice that the money is gone, but when the bill comes due, you'll find you have the money already in a savings account, saving you the pain of having to scrape together the money for the bill. Even better, it will have likely earned a few dollars' worth of interest—an extra bonus for being smart about your bills.

332. KNOW WHAT EVERY FEE IS ON EVERY BILL

Take a recent copy of each of your regular bills and go through them all, item by item. Try to figure out what every fee is. If you don't know what the fee is, call the company and ask what it is. Quite often, you're being assessed a fee or two that do not apply to you and your situation, and identifying them now means a few dollars each month that you get to keep in your wallet instead of needlessly sending to a company. Knowledge is money, particularly when it comes to fees.

333. ALWAYS ASK FOR FEES TO BE WAIVED

Even if you know what a fee is, if you're uncertain as to the necessity of a fee you're being charged, whether it is on a monthly bill, in a contract you're about to sign, or in a bank transaction, always ask for that fee to be waived. Your bank statement is usually a place where many useless fees stack up, but many other needless fees crop up on telephone bills, cable bills, energy bills, and so on. If you don't see the purpose of a fee, call and ask it to be waived. If you don't get a clear answer as to why it can't be waived, ask to speak to a supervisor. Getting even one fee waived, particularly a recurring fee, usually pays for the effort put out for several fees.

334. PAY YOUR BILLS ON A WEEKLY CYCLE, NOT A MONTHLY ONE

Move to a cycle of paying your bills every week instead of every month. At the end of a week, collect all of your outstanding bills and pay them all at once. This serves two purposes. First, it allows you to entirely avoid late fees and missed grace periods, which can stack unwanted charges on future bills. Second, if you find yourself a little short during one session of bill payments, you can easily hold the bill until the following week without worrying about whether it will be late and incur more charges. A weekly cycle of bill paying can save you a great deal of money, particularly if you're consistently late with bills and have faced late charges before.

335. IF YOU KNOW YOU'RE GOING TO BE LATE ON A BILL, CALL THEM

If a situation ever arises where you know that you're going to send in a bill late, call the company and describe the situation to them, and ask for the late fee to be waived just this once. Quite often, particularly if you're a long-term customer and have consistently paid your bills on time, they'll gladly waive a late fee if you can get your bill in within a certain number of days past the due date. In a pinch, a simple phone call can often save you a penalty, keeping that money in your pocket right where it belongs.

336. Learn How to Use Online Bill Pay

One of the most effective tools available to you for paying bills is online bill pay. If your bank offers this for your use, take advantage of it, particularly if it's free. Such services are typically very easy to use. You just enter the account information for your bills once, including the address where you send the bill to and your account information, and save it in their system. Then, you basically just fill out your payments electronically on their website, entering the amount you intend to pay and identifying which company you wish to make the payment to. Click your mouse a time or two and the bill is paid immediately. No need to waste a stamp or an envelope on the bill—it's already done. If you pay six bills a month with this method, you can easily save $30 a year just in stamps and envelopes using online bill pay.

337. Schedule Regular Bills to Be Paid Automatically

Another particularly useful feature of online bill pay is the ability to schedule payments. For example, let's say you pay the same fixed amount each month for your mortgage and for your student loans. With online bill pay, you can set up these bills to be paid automatically each month a few days before they're due. Not only does this save you stamps, but it also saves you time and ensures that you won't ever be late on that particular bill, avoiding any nasty late fees that you might incur. Automatic bill payments are easily the smartest and cheapest way to take care of regular bills. Set them up once and you don't have to worry about remembering to pay the bill ever again.

CHEAP TACTIC$ FOR
VACATIONS

338. PLAN *FAR* IN ADVANCE

The best time to plan a summer vacation is during the previous summer. Not only do you have plenty of breathing room to figure out exactly what you want to do, but you can often get stellar rates reserving things far in advance as compared to reserving closer to the dates you wish to travel, and it gives you more time to keep your eyes open for good deals along the way. Plus, locking things in stone far in advance gives you much more leeway to get the time off from work and make any other necessary plans you need to make—it not only saves money, but saves you a lot of headaches, too.

339. DO YOUR OWN TRAVEL PLANNING

Instead of relying on someone else to plan a trip for you, get involved and do the planning yourself. Organize your own transportation, lodging, and tickets to any events you want to attend. With the many online tools available to you, it's easy to find good rates on these options without having to pay the expensive fees that a travel agent might charge you just for a bit of planning convenience. Make a list of what you need on your trip and take care of each category yourself, acting as your own travel agent.

340. BE FLEXIBLE WHEN YOU PLAN

If you're planning far in advance, you have lots of flexibility when it comes to the dates and locations that you'll be traveling. The more flexibility you have, the better—find out what all of the restrictions are before you even begin planning by checking on the dates that everyone can get away from their work and other commitments. Don't commit to a specific plan too quickly. Instead, ask around and gather ideas before committing to a specific plan. Tap the social network you built and see whether your friends have any suggestions or valuable resources (like, perhaps, a cabin owned by a friend of a friend) that you can utilize. Look at lots of potential options within your plan and get the whole family involved in the details. Vacation options may open up that you didn't know existed. The more flexible you are about your plans as they come together, the more likely you are to plan a vacation that everyone will thoroughly enjoy while also saving quite a bit of money on the trip.

341. CONSIDER CAMPING

One often-overlooked option is the idea of camping while traveling, particularly if your mode of transportation is a lengthy car trip. Instead of spending your vacation money on a hotel during your car trip, instead rent a campsite for the night and cut some serious expense out of your trip. You can often spend four nights or more in a tent for the cost of one night in a hotel. Don't want to camp out for your entire vacation? Go ahead and mix the two by spending a few nights camping in one place, then stay in a hotel the rest of the time.

342. Consider All Forms of Transportation, Including Train and Bus

Don't just immediately rule out all options besides flying or driving. It may be much more cost-effective to take a train or a bus to your destination and rent a car when you arrive instead of burning gas and putting wear and tear on your car during the long trip to your destination. Trains and buses can also be a low-cost alternative to airfare, particularly if you're traveling as a family. They may take a bit longer, but the cost savings can be tremendous. Include services such as Greyhound and Amtrak in your travel planning and you may just save your family some significant cash on your vacation.

343. Stay away from Tourist Traps

While it's tempting to see the "touristy" sites when you visit a place, including all of the famous landmarks and amusement parks, you're much better off if you get away from the tourist traps and instead observe how the locals live. Spend some of your trip hitting the must-see tourist sites, but then get off the beaten path and find some of the undiscovered things on your trip. Get out in the countryside and view the natural beauty of the region you're visiting. Go to some of the smaller cities and towns and enjoy some of the truly local fare. Not only will they make the trip less expensive, but going away from the tourist traps will also give you an interesting and unique vacation that goes far beyond the same old things you find in guide books.

344. Pack Food and Beverages

If you're about to embark on a long car trip, you'll always come out ahead if you pack a cooler full of beverages, snacks, and meals before you leave. Doing this enables you to stop at a park and enjoy an inexpensive meal instead of stopping at a restaurant along the way. It also allows you to dip into the cooler for a cold beverage instead of stopping at a gas station and spending your money on their expensive fare. You can do the same when returning home as well. Stop at a grocery store before you depart and stock up on food and drinks at low prices before you leave. You can even do this while you're there— eat simple meals in your hotel room or at the campground instead of bearing the big expense of dining out. Doing this even part of the time can really reduce the cost of a family vacation.

345. Explore Your Local Area

Instead of spending a lot of money on big, exciting trips, spend some of your vacations exploring your local area. Visit historical and cultural sites that you can reach and fully enjoy over a weekend. Instead of planning one megatrip, you can do three or four of these short trips in a summer and still save significant money. Don't know what to look for? Get a map and draw a circle around your area that includes everything that's two hundred miles away or less. Everything within that circle is worth looking into. Do some Internet searching on these states and counties. You'll be surprised how many interesting things you'll find, even in the most rural areas.

346. For Hotel Rooms,
Call the Local Branch and Negotiate

If you're booking hotel rooms, don't just pop onto a website and book a room at a hotel, particularly if you're reserving well in advance. Instead, get the phone number of the hotel you'd like to stay at and call them. Ask to speak to a manager (as you'll likely be unable to negotiate with the person who first answers the phone), ask what their rate is for a hotel room far in advance (providing the dates), then negotiate. Flat-out ask for a lower rate than that, and suggest you'll try a competitor. Managers usually have the flexibility to adjust rates and thus you can often end up with a discount just because you did your footwork. This works particularly well in more rural areas where the hotels rarely fill to capacity. They'll negotiate because they need the business.

347. Do Necessary Currency
Conversions Before You Leave

If you're heading to a country that uses a different currency than you, convert some cash long before you head out on your trip. Your bank may provide this service for you for a very low fee or no fee at all, and if that doesn't work, there are usually currency exchanges available in most large towns and cities. Don't ever use currency exchanges at airports, hotels, or tourist information sites. They universally have very high rates. You'll get a far better deal if you do the legwork yourself in advance of your trip.

348. Know the Rules When You Use
Your ATM Card When Abroad

Your ATM card is usually the best method you have of getting a good exchange rate when traveling abroad. Call your bank well before you travel and find out about any extra fees you'll be charged for using the card in your country of destination, particularly if you use the card as a credit card. There will probably be some fees involved, but if the fees add up to a significant amount or there are a lot of hoops to jump through, do some shopping around for a checking account at another bank that has better fees and service abroad, then put enough cash in that checking account so that you'll have plenty on your trip. A bit of legwork now can save you a pile of fees and headaches abroad.

349. Plan the Backbone of Your Vacation
Around Inexpensive Stuff

Instead of just hitting tourist attraction after tourist attraction, space them out and fill in the gaps in between with more inexpensive activities. Find out about natural attractions and state parks in the area. Are there free museums, zoos, and other such things in the area where you're going? Build up a long list of things to do in the area you're visiting that have little or no cost by reading up on the area and the resources available there, both on the Internet and at the library. A long list of inexpensive activities means that there will surely be a few things that intrigue most of the people on the trip. Use this list as the primary tool for selecting activities on your trip, maximizing the inexpensive stops and minimizing the expensive ones.

350. Avoid Typical Souvenirs

It's easy to just grab the typical souvenirs when you're traveling. A quick stop in a gift shop and you have something ready to go. The only problem is that the typical gift store item is not only overpriced, but it's also not something that would fill your recipient's heart with joy. Instead, take a serious look at the area where you are and get something local that the recipient would particularly enjoy, and that includes you. Skip the gift shop. Instead, get a bottle of the local wine, hot sauce, barbecue sauce, jelly, or another local treat (which will be far cheaper than the typical gift shop item, anyway). Get a few simple postcards and drop them in the mail instead of worrying about some "perfect" souvenir. The real purpose is to show you care, is it not? For yourself, keep a travel journal. Write down your thoughts each day in a little notebook. That little notebook will bring back many more memories than a pile of T-shirts ever will.

351. Use a Digital Camera with a Large Memory Card Instead of Film

Never travel without taking along your digital camera. Invest in a huge memory card and feel free to snap plenty of pictures. If you have a huge memory card, you can snap pictures of anything that looks interesting. Later, you can just toss out the pictures that didn't turn out well and the rest will provide a wonderful record of your memorable trip. It's also another brilliant substitute for expensive souvenirs. Instead of buying everyone back home junk that they really didn't want, spend some time taking pictures of things you think people at home might enjoy, then send them those pictures when you arrive home, or post them on a website to share with everyone.

352. USE THE "PEAK-END" RULE

One particular trait of human psychology is known as the "peak-end" rule. Our memories of something are defined by the peak of that experience and also the end of that experience. In other words, when you think back to your vacation in a year or two, you'll likely just remember the best thing you did and the very last thing you did, along with a few other scattered bits. So, when you plan your vacation, instead of jamming each day with amazing things, just plan one peak experience, the real centerpiece of your trip, and one great experience near the end of the trip, perhaps on the next-to-last or last day. Fill the rest of the trip with inexpensive options and also relaxation, and you will create an incredibly memorable vacation without shelling out the cash for nonstop and exhausting memorable activities.

353. ALIGN VACATION TRIPS WITH VISITING FAMILY AND FRIENDS

When you're traveling, particularly on a long road or train trip, devise a plan that enables you to stop and see family and friends on the long legs of the trip. Not only will this usually amount to a free night's sleep while traveling, but it's also a perfect opportunity to touch base with people you may not get to see very often. It's often worth it to plan your travel in an unorthodox way just to make it to visit family and friends. The opportunity to catch up is personally worth it and the free night of sleep makes it financially worth it.

354. DON'T OVERLOAD A VACATION WITH SCHEDULED ACTIVITIES

When you're planning a trip, it's often tempting to pencil in tons of things to do on various days because there's so much you'd like to see. This often results in expensive tickets purchased in advance, lots of pressure to stay on schedule when you arrive, and a sense of wistfulness when you see things you wish you had time to explore, but don't. Instead of planning tons of activities in advance, just plan one or two and leave the rest of the trip entirely open, so that if you're out and about and stumble upon something interesting to explore, you can just detour at your own desire. Not only is this a less expensive method for planning a trip (as exploration and discovering new things is often the cheapest part of a trip), it's also much less stressful and more fun. Don't make a tight schedule, instead, just bring along a big list of inexpensive ideas that can fit in anywhere.

355. Vacation with Others

If you're still worried about vacation costs, plan a vacation trip with another family, so that many of the costs for various activities can be split. Thinking of renting a cabin somewhere? Invite another family to come along and split the cost. You can also split the cost of car rentals, boat rentals, and other expenses that might come up during a trip, plus a well-chosen traveling companion can increase the enjoyment factor of a vacation.

ng Exchange • Never Be an Early Adopter • Insulate Your Water Heater • Start a Garden • Learn to Love Left
ter • Move to a Cheaper Neighborhood • Rent Out Unused Rooms • Check and Replace Furnace Filters • Dr
Bills on Time • Automate Your Savings • Only Wash Full Loads of Dishes or Clothes • Carpool • Air Up All o

TEN TACTIC$ FOR
STAYING CHEAP

356. Figure Out Exactly What You Saved

Whenever you use a tactic in this book to reduce your expenses, it's worthwhile to figure out exactly how much you're saving by using this tactic, as it can directly affect your budgeting for the month. Eliminated your coffee addiction? Figure up how much you used to spend on coffee. Dropped a subscription service? How much did it save you this month? If you have a good grip on your spending and know where your money is going, each frugal tactic you use will free up some amount of money that you can use for something else. Perhaps you can add it to your debt snowball if it's a recurring savings, or you can snowflake it if it's a one-time savings. The real benefit, though, is psychological. By figuring up how much you've saved by making a good choice, you'll directly translate your action into real dollars and cents, something that you can tell others about and something that you can be personally proud of.

357. Automatically Sock Away That Savings

Many people wonder what to do with their careful planning once their debts are paid off. The next step in living a life of financial freedom is not to start spending that money, but instead to start saving it. When you've paid off your mortgage, don't start spending that money; instead, start automatically saving that mortgage payment, or dabble your toes in investing. Eventually, that money will build up into something that can enable you to change your life. Maybe you've always dreamed of going back to school or trying another career. Perhaps the next time you buy a car, you can just pay cash for it instead of taking on a car loan. If you stick to your money-saving principles and sock away that money instead of spending it, you'll eventually have personal choices that you never dreamed of.

358. HANDLE A RAISE INTELLIGENTLY

When you get a raise at work, it may be tempting to celebrate and to use that money as a personal reward to buy something nice for yourself. Instead, think about the times where you were barely making ends meet and were scared of facing the next bill. Instead of using that raise to buy more stuff that you were happy not having before, use that extra money to get rid of your debt a little bit faster or to save for a big purchase, like an appliance or an automobile. Don't be tempted to spend more just because of a little bump in your income.

359. HANDLE A WINDFALL INTELLIGENTLY, TOO

What about a big bonus check or a nice inheritance? Surely, that's something you can use to live the high life, right? Think of it this way: A windfall is an opportunity to undo the mistakes of your past, not repeat them. When you receive a windfall, put it in the bank immediately. Buy a certificate of deposit at your local bank with the entire amount so you can't touch it. Then think carefully about what you can do with it. While it might be tempting to think about all of the fun you could have with the money, in the end you'll just be right back where you are right now, with the same problems and the same worries. Instead, consider using that windfall to eliminate any debt you might have, or sock it away in an investment somewhere for your children's education or for your own retirement. Sure, you might not get to have that fun you're imagining, but you'll no longer worry about that debt you've built up. Maybe you won't have to worry about how you'll pay for college for your kids, or how on earth you'll ever be able to retire and enjoy life. Instead of just spending it wildly, put that windfall to work for you.

360. FIND FRUGAL FRIENDS

It's hard to live cheap when you're constantly encouraged by your friends to spend money. How can you save money, after all, if your friends are constantly heading out to the mall? One way is to simply look for new friends who share your other interests. Try some of the socializing tips to find people who share your values. Look particularly for activities that might attract frugal people, like the film club and the book club at the library or at a volunteer project. Get to know people and suggest frugal social opportunities with them to build a friendship. It's a lot easier to be cheap if you have friends who share the same philosophy; you can constantly help each other and motivate each other to make good financial choices.

361. THINK ABOUT WHY YOU WANT SOMETHING

We all have idle desires. We think about the things that we wish we had and we're often tempted to make choices to allow us to have these desires. Instead of just thinking about how much you want something, ask yourself why you want it. Did you see an interesting advertisement? Is that advertisement realistic? Maybe you saw someone else enjoying whatever it is you're thinking about. That person might be having fun, but would you really enjoy it? Use this tactic every time you start thinking about something you want, and you'll be surprised how often that idle desire is actually working to convince you to buy something you don't really need or even want when you think about it rationally.

362. REMEMBER THAT TIME IS MONEY

One of the most common complaints about living cheap is that many money-saving tactics also can eat up a bit of time. If you're wondering how you'll ever be able to live without paying for convenience (like when eating out instead of making food at home), look for ways to save time in your own life and tackle them as fervently as you tackle ways to save money. There are countless tactics for saving time: Cut down on your television viewing, reduce the number of activities you're involved with (particularly ones that eat into your personal expenses, too), and keep a sharp eye on your personal energy level.

363. KEEP TRYING NEW CHEAP TACTICS

Just because you're turning your financial life around doesn't mean that there's no longer anything useful you can learn about living cheap. Look online at various websites that offer frugal living tips and other good financial advice, particularly those that engage you in conversation (you can start by visiting my own site, The Simple Dollar, at *www.thesimpledollar.com*). Visit the library and check out books on frugal topics. Most important of all, actually try out the ideas you learn. You might find that the most surprising things work well for you.

364. SHARE YOUR EXPERIENCES AND FRUGAL TIPS

While it's great to find new frugal tips, it's also useful to share them as well. Talk to your friends and swap frugal ideas. Search online for frugal message boards and blogs to share your ideas. Perhaps you could even start your own blog to share frugal tactics. You can get a free one at *www.blogspot.com* or *www.wordpress.com*. Putting your frugal ideas out there not only helps inspire and motivate others to be frugal, but it often inspires others to share their own frugal tactics—a win-win situation, indeed.

365. HAVE FUN

This is the most important thing of all. Have fun in whatever you choose to do, and realize that living cheap can often be incredibly enjoyable. You'll never know how much fun frugality might be until you dip your toes in and give it a shot, so flip through this book, find a tactic or two, and get started today. Not only will you discover something new to do, but you'll also save money, and that will likely help relieve some of the stress you feel about money. What could be more fun than that?

ADDITIONAL RESOURCES

For more information on these tips, additional money-saving tactics, and suggestions for additional reading, please visit this book's free companion website at:

WWW.THESIMPLEDOLLAR.COM/365